James FitzGibbon

Defender of Upper Canada

by Ruth McKenzie

Dundurn Press
Toronto and Charlottetown
1983

Editor: Blaine R. Beemer
Design and Production: Ron and Ron Design Photography
Typesetting: Q Composition Incorporated
Printing and Binding: Laflamme & Charrier Inc., Quebec, Canada

The publication of this book was made possible by support from several sources. The author and publisher wish to acknowledge the generous assistance and ongoing support of the Canada Council and the Ontario Arts Council.

J. Kirk Howard, Publisher

Dundurn Press Limited
P.O. Box 245, Station F
Toronto, Canada, M4Y 2L5

Canadian Cataloguing in Publication Data
McKenzie, Ruth.
James FitzGibbon: defender of Upper Canada

(Dundurn lives)
Bibliography: p.
Includes index.
ISBN 0-919670-70-9 (bound). – ISBN 0-919670-71-7 (pbk.)

1. FitzGibbon, James, 1780-1863. 2. Soldiers – Canada – Biography. 3. Canada – Officials and employees – Biography. I. Title. II. Series.

FC443.F57M44 1983 971.03'092'4 C84-098202-X
F1032.M44 1983

James FitzGibbon

Defender of Upper Canada

by Ruth McKenzie

FitzGibbon in Masonic garb

Contents

Acknowledgements

Material for this biography originated mainly in manuscript documents in the Public Archives of Canada, the Archives of Ontario, the Metropolitan Toronto Library and the Public Record Office of London, England. I am grateful to these institutions for allowing me to examine their files and for the courtesy of their personnel. I wish to thank also the Vestry Office of the Cathedral Church of St. James, Toronto, for permitting me to check early baptismal and burial records, and the Buffalo and Erie County Historical Society of Buffalo, New York, for providing information on Dr. Cyrenius Chapin.

In tracing James FitzGibbon's Irish background, I received generous and valuable assistance from the Right Honourable Desmond Fitz-Gerald, Knight of Glin; John FitzGibbon and his daughter Mary, of Glin, Ireland; Robert Cussen, Newcastle West, Ireland; Edward Keane, formerly of the National Library of Ireland, Dublin; and from officers of the Genealogical Office, the Public Record Office and the Registry of Deeds, Dublin. My very warm thanks go to Major-General Sir Edmund Hakewell-Smith, Governor of the Military Knights of Windsor, and to Colonel and Mrs. A. E. Clark, through whose courtesy I was privileged to visit a military knight's house in Windsor Castle; also to Mrs. Elliot FitzGibbon of Ashtead, Surrey, England for her friendly assistance and hospitality.

Of the many Canadians who assisted me in various ways, I can mention only a few. I am particularly indebted to the following: the family of the late C. Gwyllym Dunn of Ste Pétronille, Quebec, great-great-grandchildren of James FitzGibbon, who generously gave me access to all the FitzGibbon memorabilia in their possession; Professor J. K. Johnson of Carleton University, Ottawa, for his early encouragement to write the biography of James FitzGibbon; Lorna Proctor, Archivist of the Women's Canadian Historical Society of Toronto, for putting the FitzGibbon papers in the Society's collection at my disposal; and George Waters, formerly Curator of Fort York, for showing me around old Fort York and giving me documentation on the early days when FitzGibbon lived there. To all of the above, my sincere thanks and appreciation.

Ruth McKenzie

Chapter One

Introduction: The Hero as Public Servant

One of the ironies of history is that James FitzGibbon, the hero of the Battle of Beaver Dams in 1813, is now remembered, if at all, as the British officer to whom Laura Secord delivered her warning of the impending American attack. There is the irony also that FitzGibbon, who was one of the first to sense the danger of armed rebellion in 1837, who led the attack on the rebels at Montgomery's Tavern and who was credited by the citizens of Toronto for saving the city from the rebels, has been overshadowed in accounts of the rebellion by Sir Allan MacNab, the colourful and dynamic politician who actually served *under* Colonel FitzGibbon on the march to Montgomery's.

In the decade preceding the rebellion, James FitzGibbon, then clerk of the House of Assembly in Upper Canada (Ontario), was the object of more than one vitriolic attack by William Lyon Mackenzie in the pages of his *Colonial Advocate*. Mackenzie saw FitzGibbon as one of the "snug little nest of clerks and other public servants for hire"[1] who, through the patronage of the lieutenant-governor, held a plurality of offices. When Mackenzie was in London in 1832, campaigning to have Sir John Colborne recalled from his post as lieutenant-governor of Upper Canada, he singled out FitzGibbon as an example of Colborne's favouritism. Writing to Lord Goderich, secretary of state for the colonies, Mackenzie listed FitzGibbon's various appointments: "Clerk of the House of Assembly, Chairman of the Quarter Sessions, registrar of the Court of Probate, Superintendant of College Buildings, Justice of the Peace &c".[2]

Mackenzie was noted for exaggeration, but here he spoke the truth. FitzGibbon held those offices and more, and he owed his positions to two lieutenant-governors, Sir Peregrine Maitland and Sir John Colborne. It was Maitland who first appointed FitzGibbon justice of the peace, Home District, and it was Maitland who made him clerk of the House of Assembly and registrar of the Court of Probate. FitzGibbon retained those positions under Colborne, and was entrusted with other responsibilities as well.

Despite the patronage of the two lieutenant-governors, FitzGibbon never succeeded in gaining entrance to the inner circle of government. His political sympathies were appropriately conservative, and his loyalty to the Crown unquestioned, but he remained an outsider to the governing clique that became known as the Family Compact.

James FitzGibbon's struggle for advancement began in the British army, where he was, even then, an outsider – Irish, poor, and lacking the military tradition. In the eighteenth century, the Irish were not viewed favourably by the British army. Until 1756, no Irishman was accepted as a volunteer in the army, and no Irish Catholic until 1799. As the son of a poor man, James could not buy an officer's commission. He had to start at the bottom of the military hierarchy and depend on his own wits for promotion, which meant impressing his commanding officers. In this, he succeeded very well, but only up to a point.

When FitzGibbon became a public servant in Upper Canada, his career was conditioned by the system of patronage and appointments that prevailed. Like all public servants he had to accommodate his talents and efforts to the circumstances of the time. Thus his career illustrates the way in which the public service of Upper Canada operated.

Two questions of particular significance arise. Why was FitzGibbon unsuccessful in obtaining an important government post, such as he desired? And to what extent was his career limited by his place as an outsider – a person born outside the province, and with no United Empire Loyalist connections?

For reasons that will emerge as FitzGibbon's life story unfolds, the man who enjoyed favours from two lieutenant-governors in the 1820s and early 1830s experienced extreme frustration in the years preceding the 1840 Act of Union and those immediately following. Strangely enough, James FitzGibbon rounded out his life in Windsor Castle.

His story begins in Ireland.

Glin Castle, Glin, Ireland

Chapter Two

Early Years in the British Army

James FitzGibbon was reared on poverty in a 15-acre farm near the village of Glin in County Limerick, Ireland. "Upon this [farm] I have dug with a spade from Monday Morning to Saturday Evening without shoes or stockings, until I inlisted [*sic*]", he recollected a half-century later.[1] Born on 16 November 1780, James was the second son of Garrett FitzGibbon and his wife Mary Widenham, in a family of seven: five boys (John, James, Thomas, Gerald and Henry) and two girls (Margaret and Anne).

The FitzGibbon holding formed part of the estate of Thomas FitzGerald, Knight of Glin, whose demesne dated back to the thirteenth century. Glin Castle, the three-storied mansion in which the Knight of Glin lived, formed the backdrop to the lives of the FitzGibbons. It stood (and may be seen today) in spacious grounds overlooking the River Shannon. The castle must have seemed the ultimate in elegance to the boy James.

The small stone house with thatched roof, where the FitzGibbons lived, was only a short distance from the banks of the Shannon. Across the river in summertime, the yellow furze shone golden in the green fields of County Clare, the distant hills merging into the sky, a view that stirred in James a sense of beauty and a love of nature.

In his boyhood, James was a voracious reader, but his choice of books was severely limited. *The History of Troy's Destruction, The Arabian Nights' Entertainment* –

such were the narratives that quickened his imagination. James was more fortunate than many, for he attended the village school until he was eleven, when he had to leave to help on the farm and in his father's small linen-weaving shop. In the long winter nights, he read by candlelight, and his father instructed him in Latin. From his youngest days, James FitzGibbon developed a love for the English language, which he learned to use with great facility, whether writing a friendly letter or a memorial to a lieutenant-governor.

Garrett (also known as Gerald) FitzGibbon was a man of independent mind. The FitzGibbons were traditionally Roman Catholic, as were almost all the families in their parish. James' branch of the family became Protestant, perhaps in 1763, when records show that a Gibbon FitzGibbon, who may have been Garrett's father, conformed to the Established Church of Ireland (comparable to the Church of England). Possibly Garrett was the first member of the family to renounce Catholicism. What is certain is that by 1786 Garrett FitzGibbon was Protestant, for in that year he obtained a 99-year lease of some property, which he could not have done as a Catholic.

The pressure to turn Protestant was very great under the Penal Laws that dominated life in Ireland. Under those laws, enacted by the British Parliament, Roman Catholics were deprived of the most basic civil rights. They could not vote in an election, hold any civil or military office, nor marry outside their faith. They were forbidden to purchase land or take a lease of more than 31-years' duration. Landlords, like the Knight of Glin, were Protestant.

The FitzGibbons were the only Protestant family in the community. Apart from his brothers and sisters, James' playmates were all Catholic. This boyhood circumstance, followed by his years in the British army where his fellow soldiers were almost all Protestant, gave James FitzGibbon a sympathy and tolerance for both religious groups which led him, as a mature man in Upper Canada, to work for peace between the Roman Catholics and the Orange Protestants.

By the time James was sixteen, the Napoleonic storm clouds had begun to gather over Europe, threatening to spread over Great Britain and Ireland. In the summer of 1796, Napoleon Bonaparte rapidly conquered Italy. Even in faraway Glin, the people were alarmed, for they lived where the Shannon widened to join the Atlantic Ocean and could be entered by an alien fleet. There was a flurry of military preparations throughout Ireland. The large landowners organized yeomanry corps to protect their lives and property and the lives of their tenants. When the Knight of Glin formed his corps, Garrett FitzGibbon signed up for himself and his two eldest sons, John and James.

Just before Christmas 1796, the worst fears of the Irish seemed to be realized when the French fleet entered Bantry Bay, a deep inlet on the southwest coast of Ireland. Fortunately, the invasion was defeated by the weather. Most of the French ships were dispersed by winds and fog before they reached the bay. The remainder returned to France without landing or firing a shot. Meanwhile, the British army arrived in southern Ireland. An English sergeant and two privates were billeted in the FitzGibbon cottage, causing some trepidation on the part of the family. James, like all Irish boys in those days, had learned to hate and fear the English. Now, to his surprise, he found that the three English soldiers were very likeable. The sergeant often drilled the FitzGibbon boys in the evening in the stone-paved kitchen, and James responded with enthusiasm. He decided that he wanted to be a soldier. In the Knight of Glin's yeomanry corps, he learned the military drill quickly, and soon the commander began to rely on him to put the men through their exercises. Though only 17, James was promoted to sergeant over the heads of many older men, including his father and brother.

Two more invasion scares led to the formation of new military units for the defence of Ireland. Sergeant FitzGibbon was recruited into one of them, the Loyal Tarbert Infantry (Fencibles), founded by Colonel Sir Edward Leslie. Unlike the yeomanry regiments, which were of local origin and for local defence only, the fencibles received their commissions from the British Crown and could be called upon to serve anywhere in the British Isles. Thus it came about that in 1799, James FitzGibbon's regiment was transferred to England. Before long, the tall lanky sergeant was induced to enlist in the British army, despite his promise to his mother that he would never do so. The bounty of four pounds four shillings that the British army offered to volunteers proved to be irresistible to the shilling-a-day sergeant. There was also, of course, the tempting thought of seeing faraway places and participating in exciting events.

In August, James joined the 49th Regiment of Foot, the Hertfordshires, in the south of England. There he came under two officers who would be influential in his career: Major John Vincent, his commanding officer, and Lieutenant-Colonel Isaac Brock, commander of the regiment. Colonel Brock would become his exemplar and his patron.

Isaac Brock was born in Guernsey in 1769, the same year in which two world-famous generals were born, Napoleon Bonaparte and the Duke of Wellington. At the age of 15, Brock purchased an ensign's commission in the 8th Regiment. He rose rapidly through the ranks, purchasing his commissions as was the custom, and within 13 years became senior lieutenant-colonel of the 49th Regiment. That was in 1797, two years before James FitzGibbon joined the regiment as a sergeant. At 30 years of age, Brock was a distinguished looking man of martial bearing, over six feet tall, erect, athletic, with handsome features, courteous and pleasing in manner. Brock was a natural leader of men, though he exacted from them a high standard of behaviour and discipline.

Nineteen-year-old James FitzGibbon experienced his baptism of fire in the battle of Egmond-aan-Zee, Holland, on 7 October, 1799. The day brought a surprise ending for the eager young soldier. The 49th Regiment had landed on the beach at the Helder about a month earlier, joining the first division of the British expeditionary force which, with the Russians, aimed to dislodge the French from Holland. The men of the 49th, encamped on the dunes, had waited impatiently for the summons to battle. When it came, on 7 October, they assembled on the beach before daylight, ready to advance. Altogether the force totalled some 29,000 infantry and 1,500 cavalry. Colonel Brock supervised the deployment of his regiment on the beach and then left. FitzGibbon found that his unit was to be commanded by Lieutenant-Colonel Roger Hale Sheaffe, an officer who had served ten years in Canada and would return there to become a controversial figure before and during the War of 1812. On this, his first day of battle, James was to act as a supernumerary sergeant with no particular responsibility except to observe.

As the column marched north, with the North Sea on its left and the sand-hills on its right, the soldiers found walking difficult and dangerous. Behind the patches of scrub growing on the dunes, enemy sharpshooters lurked. James was amazed at the confusion of the battle, shocked when one of his fellows was shot, and surprised at the apparent lack of heroism in those around him. Only one man made an indelible impression on him. That was Colonel Brock's brother, John Savery, the paymaster of the regiment who was acting as aide-de-camp to General Sir Ralph Abercromby. James watched in amazement as Savery Brock passed from the top of one sand-hill to another, talking to the men and encouraging them, in apparent disregard of the danger. James resolved to follow Savery's example: he would be the first to advance when the occasion arose. His resolution was put to the test that very afternoon.

Around five p.m., a group of French soldiers emerged from a valley near the spot where Sergeant FitzGibbon and his comrades happened to be. The Frenchmen charged up a sand-hill, waving their hats and swords in the face of gunfire. Thinking at first that they were Dutch soldiers who wished to surrender, as some had done already, the British officer ordered the men to cease firing. FitzGibbon, emulating Savery Brock, went forward to meet the approaching soldiers. Fearlessly he disarmed two of them. Suddenly he found himself seized by the collar, his pike wrenched from him, and two bayonets prodding him in the back. The French soldiers dragged him over the sand-hill, a prisoner of war. James was stripped, searched and robbed of his greatcoat, his homespun linen shirt and the money in his pocket – an inglorious end to his first day of battle.

Along with a hundred other prisoners, James had to march for 15 days to Valenciennes in northern France, where he was imprisoned. Relieved that he was not placed in a dungeon, as his over-wrought imagination had anticipated, James made the best of his imprisonment by learning to communicate in French. He was released in January of the following year as part of a prisoner-of-war exchange, and returned to England. (The British had won the Battle of Egmond-aan-Zee but later, by the convention of Alkmaar, had agreed to withdraw from Holland).

A year later, FitzGibbon's army career took an unexpected turn when, with a detachment of his regiment, he joined the Baltic naval expedition as a marine. His ship, the *Monarch*, led the fleet on its passage from the Kattegat through the narrow strip of water that separates Denmark from Sweden, past Kronborg Castle (the scene of Shakespeare's *Hamlet*), and into the Oresund (the Sound), on which Copenhagen is situated. This was the prelude to the Battle of Copenhagen, a fierce naval engagement between the British and the Danes that was won by the British through the strategy of Admiral Lord Nelson. (This was the occasion when Nelson looked through the telescope with his blind eye, refusing to see Admiral Sir Hyde Parker's signal to retreat). Although the *Monarch* suffered heavier losses than any other ship, James FitzGibbon escaped unharmed. (Years later he received the Naval General Service Medal as a reward for his service at Copenhagen). The badly damaged *Monarch* was sent back to England for repairs, and the marines were transferred to the *Elephant*.

On this ship, an incident occurred that brought FitzGibbon to Colonel Brock's attention for the first time. Brock was not with the marines, however. The detachment from the 49th was under the command of Colonel William Hutchinson, an officer of less patience and understanding than Brock. Soon he became displeased with James FitzGibbon.

One morning, Colonel Hutchinson summoned Sergeant FitzGibbon to appear on deck. James had to get dressed, and by the time he arrived on deck Hutchinson was in an angry mood. He reprimanded FitzGibbon sharply while the other soldiers and sailors stood by. James felt humiliated. Rather than suffer such treatment again, he took an unusual step. That evening he told Colonel

Hutchinson that he wished to retire to the ranks as a private. The colonel gave his consent.

The marines rejoined the rest of their regiment at Colchester, England, later in the summer of 1801. Colonel Brock thanked them, on parade, for their good behaviour while with the Navy and for the bravery they had shown in the Battle of Copenhagen. Then he summoned FitzGibbon. Why, Brock inquired, had he asked to be reduced to the rank of private? James told his story. But, Brock said, Colonel Hutchinson had considered the request an insult directed towards him. FitzGibbon denied any such intention. Brock persuaded James to apologize to Hutchinson, after which he was reinstated as sergeant. This being accomplished, FitzGibbon went to thank Colonel Brock for his kindness. Then he asked if he might express his views on discipline. The surprised Colonel Brock agreed to listen. In his opinion, James said, it was a mistake for an officer to censure non-commissioned officers in the presence of the privates, for it weakened authority and created ill-feeling towards the commanding officer. Brock showed no anger at this outburst. It would not be long before he would have occasion again to recognize in James FitzGibbon a very unusual sergeant.

It happened the following winter when the 49th was stationed in Chelmsford, England, and FitzGibbon was acting as pay-sergeant for his company of grenadiers. James discovered one day that his pay-sheet for February was short by one pound, 15 shillings. He was alarmed and frightened. Would he be reduced to the ranks? Would he suffer that ultimate degradation of being flogged before the other soldiers? Characteristically, James made an impulsive decision: he would present his case to the highest court of appeal, His Royal Highness, Frederick Augustus, Duke of York and Albany, commander-in-chief of the British army. He obtained a three-day pass to go to London "on business", walked the 50 kilometres from Chelmsford, and took a room at the Anchor and Vines Tavern near the Horse Guards. Tired though he was, he sat down that night and wrote a letter to the Duke of York explaining about the shortage in funds and asking to be permitted to repay the money without letting Colonel Brock know of the deficiency. James added, diplomatically, that he regarded Colonel Brock as the father of the regiment and he did not want to lose his colonel's good opinion.

Next morning, FitzGibbon went to the Horse Guards and handed his letter to the orderly on duty. While waiting for a response, he paced anxiously up and down in front of the Horse Guards. No reply came, though he waited all day. It occurred to him that some officious person might have withheld his letter from the Duke, so that night he wrote another one, making reference to his first letter, and repeating his plea. Early next morning he went again to the Horse Guards but this time he waited for the Duke of York to appear, saluted him smartly and handed him the letter. The Duke, a popular and genial prince, was taken aback, but he accepted the letter without comment and passed into the building. Before long, FitzGibbon was summoned inside. There he was ushered into a waiting-room where a colonel appeared carrying the two letters in his hand. He brought no reassuring message, but simply informed FitzGibbon that the commander-in-chief could not act without reference to Colonel Brock. "But that is what I wished to avoid", James protested. The officer insisted that this was the rule, but assured the sergeant that if he would return to his regiment he would not be treated harshly.

James resolved to return to Chelmsford the next day, but that evening he went to the theatre and, while returning to his room on foot, got soaked in a downpour. He wakened with a bad cold and fever, in no condition for a 50-kilometre walk. It was the last day of his leave, so he sent a note of explanation to the London agents of the regiment, asking them to forward it to Chelmsford. That afternoon James was astonished when two callers were announced: Colonel Isaac Brock and an accompanying officer. Brock, who had come to London that day, had happened to be at the regimental agents' office when FitzGibbon's note had arrived. He had then gone to the Horse Guards where he was given FitzGibbon's two letters to the Duke of York. His interest was now thoroughly aroused and he decided to call on the young sergeant.

James was nearly overcome with emotion when the kindly Brock, urging him to return to the regiment as soon as possible, laid a half-guinea on the table in case he might run out of money. Ironically, James discovered on his return to the regiment that the missing sum had been found, or rather had never been lost. It had only appeared so through a bookkeeping error.

From this time on, Colonel Brock began to show a special interest in James FitzGibbon, perhaps detecting in him the capacity for personal initiative combined with an agile mind. For the next ten years, as long as Brock commanded the 49th Regiment, he treated James as his protégé.

The regiment landed at Quebec in August 1802 as part of the British policy to strengthen the defences of British North America in case of war with the United States. The Americans were openly sympathetic to the French in the European war and the British feared that the United States might attack the colonies to the north. On arrival in Canada, Colonel Brock promoted Fitz-Gibbon to sergeant-major with the duties of staff-sergeant. His rate of pay rose to two shillings (50 cents) a day. James was then 22, a tall, well-built young man with lively gray eyes, a prominent nose and a determined chin. He radiated exuberance, and this, combined with his good-natured wit and exceptional strength (which he attributed to his early farming activity) made him popular with his fellow soldiers. His keen mind, alertness in observation and innate shrewdness helped to compensate for his limited schooling.

As staff-sergeant, FitzGibbon worked closely with Colonel Brock, on one occasion accompanying him across Lake Ontario from Fort York, where the regiment was then stationed, to find deserters who had fled to the United States. When some soldiers mutinied at Fort George on the Niagara River, FitzGibbon went with Brock on his mission to quell the mutiny. After the court-martial, which took place in the old Jesuits' Barracks in Quebec, Brock entrusted his staff-sergeant with the responsibility of conveying the report on the trial from Quebec to York (Toronto), where Lieutenant-General Peter Hunter, commander of the forces, resided. This 800-kilometre journey

Sir Isaac Brock

was made in January 1804, in a one-horse sleigh, through snow and long tracts of forest inhabited only by wild animals and birds.

FitzGibbon was devoted to Colonel Brock, whom he regarded as his ideal officer. Brock encouraged him to improve his education in order to qualify for officer rank. Years later, FitzGibbon recalled in a letter to Brock's nephew and biographer, Ferdinand Brock Tupper, that when he became a sergeant-major, "I then did not know the difference between a verb and a noun! but I had read much, chiefly silly Romances sold in Ireland to the peasantry, and some Ancient History". He then related a significant incident.

> In Sept. 1802, in this city [Montreal], Col. B. dictated to me while I wrote for him in the orderly Room. On writing his last word I had to pronounce it that he may proceed. At one moment the last word was "ascertain" which I pronounced "ascerten", when he turned (for he was walking to and fro in the Room) and said ascertain, young man! At that time my ignorance of my real deficiencies was very great, and I thought myself quite sufficient master of the language. But this discovery of one error roused me, and I went into Town the same day and bought a Grammar and a Dictionary, Books which I had never even seen before, and on studying them I was amazed at my great ignorance of every thing which the Grammar taught. For, altho' I could write and speak pretty accurately, because I had read so much, yet of grammar, technically, I knew absolutely nothing.[2]

Brock told FitzGibbon that he intended to recommend him for an adjutancy, saying, "I not only desire to procure for you a commission but I also wish to have you qualify yourself to take your place among gentlemen. Here are my Books, make good use of them".[3] And FitzGibbon did just that, studying diligently in his spare time.

FitzGibbon was rewarded with a commission as ensign, in February 1806. Later the duties of adjutant (an assistant to officers) were added. Brock obtained the commission for his protégé without purchase. Ordinarily, James would have had to pay £400 (roughly $2,000) for the commission, a sum far beyond the reach of a sergeant-major who earned two shillings a day. Even so, the promotions to ensign and adjutant plunged FitzGibbon into debt by £150, the cost of his uniform and equipment, including a horse which he required in his role as adjutant. This debt marked the beginning of James FitzGibbon's financial troubles. At the time, however, his future in the army looked promising. Three years later he rose to lieutenant, again through Brock's initiative, without purchase. In the ordinary course of events, this promotion would have cost £150, the difference between the price of a lieutenant's commission and the sale of an ensign's. Unfortunately, there was no vacancy for a lieutenant in the 49th Regiment so FitzGibbon had to continue to serve as adjutant.

The detachment of the 49th to which FitzGibbon belonged was transferred to Lower Canada (Quebec) in 1804, and for eight years James lived, at different periods of time, in Montreal, Quebec and Trois-Rivières. Afterwards, he looked back upon those years as happy ones. Always congenial and outgoing, he made many friends among the people of the province, among them a young girl named Mary Haley, who would become his wife some years later.

As the threat of war with the United States increased, changes of great significance took place in Upper Canada. In 1810, Brock was placed in command of all the troops in that province. He was promoted to major-general the following June, and in October 1811 he became president and administrator (provisional lieutenant-governor in the absence of Francis Gore) of Upper Canada. General Brock had the twofold responsibility of administering the civil affairs of the province and commanding the military forces. For Lieutenant FitzGibbon, Brock's new status meant an irreparable loss. Never again would he have a commanding officer who would take a special interest in him and his career.

Conscious of the change in his fortune, Lieutenant FitzGibbon wrote to Colonel John Vincent, who was then commanding the 49th Regiment, asking that he be permitted to resign as adjutant. "To personal exertions I look principally for further success in the Army", he explained, and consequently, he said, he would like more time to study and prepare himself for advancement.[4] Colonel Vincent was agreeable but there was still no vacancy for a lieutenant. In August a vacancy occurred, and FitzGibbon was relieved at last of his duties as adjutant. By that time the dreaded war between Great Britain and the United States had become a reality.

Chapter Three

Hero of the Battle of Beaver Dams

James FitzGibbon had seen no fighting since the Battle of Copenhagen, and the 31-year-old lieutenant was eager to get into action. His first assignment came in August 1812, when he escorted a brigade of 24 boats containing ordnance stores from Montreal to Kingston. While this expedition lacked the excitement and danger of battle, it required courage and skill, for the convoy had to navigate the St. Lawrence rapids and pass in full view of the American side of the river for over 160 kilometres. FitzGibbon delivered the munitions safely in Kingston and then returned with the empty boats to Montreal, only to find that the 49th Regiment had been ordered to Kingston. There he was stationed for the next four months.

General Brock won the hearts of the Upper Canadians by an unexpected early victory at Detroit in August, when an American army, under the command of Brigadier-General William Hull, surrendered without a fight to Brock's much smaller force of British regulars, Canadian militia and Indians. Brock skilfully used bluff to achieve the surrender. He sent an advance warning to Hull that the Indians of his force would be uncontrollable in battle. Then he spaced his troops so that on their march against Detroit they appeared to be a much larger force. The resulting victory did wonders for the morale of the Upper Canadians. The British government rewarded Brock with a knighthood.

Two months after the Detroit victory, a crucial battle

took place on Queenston Heights. On the morning of 13 October the Americans crossed the Niagara River in small boats from Lewiston to Queenston, where they climbed the precipice by an old overgrown and neglected path, and occupied the heights. General Brock hastened to the scene from Fort George. Brock led his troops up the heights from the village, but he had not gone far before he was killed by a sharpshooter's bullet. His aide-de-camp, Lieutenant-Colonel John Macdonell, led a second attack, but he too was fatally wounded. The troops retreated down the hill. That afternoon, Major-General Roger Hale Sheaffe, the late General Brock's second-in-command, turned defeat into victory. Taking a roundabout route through the farmland back of the village, his army of British and Canadians gained the heights to the left of the Americans, taking them by surprise. They were in a hopeless position on the edge of the precipice, and after a brief battle the Americans surrendered. Although part of the 49th Regiment participated in the day's action, Lieutenant James FitzGibbon was not with them. He remained in Kingston. The news of Brock's death must have come as a tremendous shock to him, but he did not record his feelings on the occasion. Thirty-five years later he told Ferdinand Brock Tupper, that General Brock "had been more than a father to me in that regiment which he ruled like a father".[1]

The battle that brought a hero's fame to James FitzGibbon came in June 1813. His activity that year began in January when he conducted a brigade of 45 sleighs with military supplies from Kingston to Niagara, over some 370 windswept snowy kilometres. The war turned serious in late April when York (now Toronto) fell to the Americans, and a month later Fort George met the same fate. Brigadier-General John Vincent's force at Fort George, greatly outnumbered by about 4,000 American invaders, suffered severe losses in wounded and killed. On 27 May he gave orders for the fort to be evacuated and the ammunition destroyed. Then he retreated with his army to John DeCew's house near Beaver Dams, where he ordered all the forces of the Niagara area to assemble. This post was a fine, substantial two-storey limestone house, built by John DeCew shortly before the war and lent by him to the British for use as a supply depot during the war. Lieutenant James FitzGibbon, with his small detachment of men, joined the other detachments that gathered at DeCew's house.

General Vincent continued his retreat next day, with all the forces he had assembled – a total of 1,600 regulars and fencibles – and set up his camp at Burlington Heights, at the head of Lake Ontario. His retreat left the Niagara frontier open to the Americans. Their ships held sway over Lake Ontario, and their troops outnumbered the British by two to one.

The situation became critical on 5 June when 3,500 Americans with 150 cavalry advanced to Stoney Creek and made camp on James Gage's farm, just 11 kilometres southeast of Burlington Heights. The British hastily reconnoitered the American camp although accounts vary as to how this was done. According to one version, which may be legend, James FitzGibbon accomplished the feat in the disguise of a settler, gaining entrance to the camp with a basket of butter on his arm. While he offered the butter for sale, he glanced around the camp and noted the distribution of troops and guards.[2] Whatever means were used to reconnoitre the American camp, the British officers concluded that the Americans were poorly organized and that a surprise attack should be made immediately.

On the night of 5 June some 700 British soldiers of the 8th and 49th Regiments marched silently along the road to Stoney Creek, under the command of Lieutenant-Colonel John Harvey, second-in-command to Vincent. FitzGibbon had a company of the 49th under his charge, and he was in the thick of the fighting that took place that night. According to a vivid account that he wrote the next day to his friend, the Reverend James Somerville of Montreal, the battle scene was one of great noise and confusion in the blackness of night. When the fighting came to an end, two American brigadier-generals had surrendered and 100 prisoners had been captured. General Vincent had been thrown from his horse and was lost in the woods. He did not turn up until noon the next day.[3] Neither side could claim a clear victory until the day after the battle, when British ships on Lake Ontario, under the direction of Sir James Yeo, shelled the American camp and destroyed boatloads of their supplies coming from Niagara. With their line of communications threatened, the Americans retreated to Fort George, withdrew their outposts from Fort Erie, Chippawa and Queenston, and so yielded the ascendancy on the Niagara frontier to the British.

General Vincent pursued the Americans to Forty Mile Creek (Grimsby) but no farther. He returned to his encampment on Burlington Heights. Lieutenant FitzGibbon was disappointed, even disgusted, by this lack of aggressiveness. The general's inaction, as well as the absurd incident when he got lost in the woods, left FitzGibbon with the impression that Vincent was "at all times a feeble man, both in mind and body".[4] FitzGibbon became impatient and devised his own scheme for harassing the enemy:

> This tardiness [in advancing on the Americans] suggested to me the idea of offering myself to serve in advance of the Army with 50 Chosen men to be employed where and how I might please. On the 12th I applied to Lt. Col. Harvey who readily accepted my offer and procured an Order for my immediate departure. I marched forward that night at Ten, having during the day transferred the Company to another officer, for my new men were chosen from the several Companies by myself, and I knew the men well.[5]

DeCew's stone house, their headquarters was ideally situated for partisan forays. It commanded a view of the surrounding area and gave access to roads leading north to Twelve Mile Creek (St. Catharines), northeast to Queenston and Fort George, and southeast to Niagara Falls and Chippawa. Hiding-places were plentiful in woods and ravines.

Only eleven days intervened before the Battle of Beaver Dams, but in those few days the bold and exciting deeds of FitzGibbon and his partisans gave rise to legends. It was said that the partisans practised the art of fighting in the woods in the Indian manner; that they used cow-bells for signalling; and that they were nicknamed "the Green Tigers" – "green" from the colour of

FitzGibbon took up headquarters in this stone dwelling, the DeCew house, before the Battle of Beaver Dams

their tunic facings, and "tigers" in tribute to their fierceness in fighting.

Romantic though the legends are, FitzGibbon and his "Green Tigers" actually had serious objectives in mind: to observe and report on movements of the enemy; to ferret out persons living on the Niagara frontier who were assisting the enemy; and to intercept American raiders intent upon seizing food supplies or capturing some of the inhabitants. Lieutenant FitzGibbon acted under instructions from Colonel John Harvey, deputy adjutant-general as well as second-in-command to General Vincent. Harvey warned him not to permit "the excesses to which men removed from the wholesome restraint of discipline may be expected to give way", and reminded him that however brilliant his success might be, his reputation could be effaced by acts of plunder. At the same time, Colonel Harvey held out the enticing promise that if FitzGibbon and his men conducted themselves honourably and with success against the enemy, the venture could not fail "of opening to you and those acting under you, suitable honours and rewards".[6]

The American troops of the Niagara frontier were then encamped at Fort George. One regiment only was stationed at Queenston, but it too was withdrawn to the fort on 21 June. Yet all was not peaceful. The farmers of the area were subjected to raids by parties in search of food for the American soldiers and their horses. Worse still, the raiders took as prisoners 50 or more of the able-bodied men (the Reverend Robert Addison, rector of Niagara, was one) to prevent them from serving in the militia or otherwise helping the British. Also, it was known that certain disloyal citizens, such as Joseph Willcocks, were assisting the American raiders. FitzGibbon's partisans aimed to stop such raids. In particular they hoped to trap the leading raider, Major Cyrenius Chapin of Buffalo, and his own troop of 50 mounted riflemen.

Chapin was a frontiersman – bold, independent, defiant of authority. A New Englander by birth, he had become a pioneer doctor in Buffalo, and was known to have ridden hundreds of miles on both sides of the border, treating Indians and whites alike. His familiarity with the roads and trails on the Upper Canadian side of Lake

Erie and the Niagara River served him well as leader of the raiders. Chapin's avowed purpose was to clear the frontier of persons unfriendly to the United States and to protect the inhabitants from the outrages of the British. Naturally, the Canadian settlers of the area did not take kindly to Chapin's so called "protection".

Several clashes occurred between FitzGibbon's partisans and Chapin's raiders, but the incident that attracted the greatest attention, and that may have been a factor in the American decision to attack FitzGibbon's post at DeCew's house, took place on 21 June. On that day FitzGibbon and his men went in pursuit of Chapin's riflemen who were said to be proceeding from Fort George to Chippawa. On arrival at Niagara Falls, FitzGibbon learned that 150 American infantrymen had joined the riflemen, so he took the precaution of leaving his band of men hidden in the woods while he went on alone to reconnoitre. As he rode along Lundy's Lane, Mrs. James Kerby, wife of a militia captain, ran out to warn him that she had seen the Americans disappear around the next corner. FitzGibbon soon caught sight of a horse, presumably belonging to one of Chapin's riflemen, standing riderless at Defield's Inn on the Portage Road (now Main Street of Niagara Falls) near Lundy's Lane. Dismounting, FitzGibbon was about to enter the inn to find the rifleman when suddenly an American infantryman appeared. FitzGibbon faced a levelled musket. In one quick movement he seized the musket and ordered the American to surrender. But just then the rifleman sprang out of the tavern and aimed *his* gun at FitzGibbon. Again, FitzGibbon grabbed for the gun, but now he was locked in struggle with two men. One of them seized FitzGibbon's sword and was about to use it when the innkeeper's wife ran out, grabbed hold of the American and prevented him from wielding the sword. The upshot was that Lieutenant FitzGibbon rode off with two American prisoners and the rifleman's horse. When the account of this episode appeared in the newspapers, it delighted the besieged inhabitants of the Niagara area, and FitzGibbon's reputation as a fearless and crafty partisan began to grow.

Chapin, of course, gave a somewhat different version

of the story. "While my party was halted", he wrote after the war, "we were attacked by that wiley [*sic*] officer, FitzGibbon. We soon beat off FitzGibbon's party and routed them, but making a rapid movement to save my men, one of them who was more slack than his fellows, by his own negligence or indolence was taken prisoner". Chapin added, significantly, "I returned to the Fort and made my report to Gen. Dearborn".[7]

Two days later, Lieutenant-Colonel Charles Boerstler of the American army, stationed at Fort George, received orders from Major-General Henry Dearborn, the American commander-in-chief in Upper Canada, to march against the British outpost at DeCew's house, to destroy the house and, if possible, to capture the enemy. General Dearborn may have wanted simply to get rid of the troublesome partisans; or he may have hoped that by wiping out FitzGibbon's post, the way would be clear to attack the other British outposts farther north, one at Twenty Mile Creek (Jordan), commanded by Lieutenant-Colonel Cecil Bisshopp, and the other under Major P.W. De Haren near Ten Mile Creek (Homer), 11 kilometres north of DeCew's. The immediate objective, according to the report of the American inquiry into the Battle of Beaver Dams that was held in Baltimore in 1815, was "to batter down Decoos [*sic*] stone house, said to be fortified, and garrisoned by a company of regulars and 60 or 100 Indians, and capture or dislodge the enemy stationed there".[8] The Americans knew of the other two British outposts but they were unaware of the size of the Indian encampment near DeCew's house. Instead of the supposed 60 or 100 Indians, there were nearly 400, consisting of a party of 180 from Lower Canada, led by Captain Dominique Ducharme, and an assemblage of 200 Six Nations and other Indians of Upper Canada, under the command of Captain William Johnson Kerr.

After dark on the evening of 23 June Colonel Boerstler began his march from Fort George to Beaver Dams with a force of over 500 men including detachments of infantry from three regiments, a company of light artillery under Captain Andrew McDowell, 20 dragoons and about 40 of Major Chapin's mounted militia. They arrived at Queenston about eleven p.m. and remained there for the night, observing the utmost precautions of silence and darkness.

Early next morning, the Americans resumed their march. They had 20 kilometres to cover. It was a hot June day and Boerstler did not permit the men to stop for refreshments. They were weary by the time they reached the beechwoods near Beaver Dams. Suddenly shots rang out. Indians seemed to be everywhere, firing from behind trees. Ambush! Colonel Boerstler was wounded in the thigh early in the battle but continued resolutely to lead his troops. After three hours of fighting, the men were nearly exhausted. Many had been wounded or killed. Ammunition was running low and no reinforcements could be expected. The hard-pressed Americans managed at last to push the Indians back a short distance to an open field. Colonel Boerstler resolved to make a final desperate charge in an effort to gain the road and retreat to Fort George.

Just then the Americans saw a British officer approaching on horseback, a white handkerchief hoisted on his musket. It was the leader of the partisans, the man they had hoped to capture, Lieutenant James FitzGibbon. Colonel Boerstler sent Captain McDowell to meet him. This is how Boerstler described the negotiations that followed:

> FitzGibbon stated that we were far outnumbered; that we could not possibly escape and that they had a number of Indians from the Northwest, by no means as easily controlled as those from the vicinity, and having suffered very severely they were outrageous and would commence a general massacre; he was therefore desirous to save the effusion of blood and demanded a surrender. He was told that we knew how to die, and they should hear from us in a few minutes. He returned very shortly, repeating the summons, and added that if we did not believe we were outnumbered and could not possibly escape, an officer would be permitted to view their troops.[9]

When the American officer went to view the British troops, he was met by a British officer who refused to let him inspect the troops. Boerstler consulted his officers

Laura Secord as an elderly woman

about the next step. They decided, in order to save bloodshed, to surrender. FitzGibbon and Boerstler then agreed upon terms.

At this point, Major De Haren arrived and "by an amazing blunder", as FitzGibbon said, nearly nullified the latter's craftily arranged terms. De Haren began to negotiate with Colonel Boerstler, until warned by FitzGibbon that "these men are my prisoners". As the Americans troops lined up to surrender their arms, De Haren indicated that they should march through the British ranks and "ground their arms on the other side". In so doing the Americans would have seen that they far outnumbered the British. They might even have refused to surrender. The quick-witted FitzGibbon said to De Haren, within hearing of the Americans, "Do you think it prudent to march them through with arms in their hands in the presence of the Indians"? Upon which, Colonel Boerstler entreated that they be permitted to lay down their arms at once.[10]

And thus it came about that 462 Americans with field-guns and ammunition surrendered to FitzGibbon and his 40-odd men. After the surrender, the Americans saw that they had been duped. The British officer, Captain John Hall, who had refused to show his troops to the American officer, had with him a mere dozen dragoons. His refusal had been prompted by Lieutenant FitzGibbon. The Irish officer had pulled off a daring coup.

How had he managed it? Although Colonel Boerstler had made every effort to preserve secrecy on the march to Beaver Dams, FitzGibbon had learned of the American plan. Laura Secord had brought the warning two days before the battle. FitzGibbon confirmed this later in three certificates that he wrote for Mrs Secord at various times (1820, 1827 and 1837) when she asked him for testimonials to support applications that she or her husband James were making for government appointments or favours. The 1827 certificate was the most specific. In it FitzGibbon stated that:

> on the 22d day of June 1813, Mrs Secord, Wife of James Secord, Esq'r . . . came to me at the Beaver Dam after Sun Set . . . and informed me that her Husband had

learnt from an American officer the preceding night that a Detachment from the American Army then in Fort George would be sent out on the following morning (the 23rd) for the purpose of Surprising and Capturing a Detachment of the 49th Regt. then at the Beaver Dam under my Command. In consequence of this information I placed the Indians . . . together with my own Detachment in a Situation to intercept the American Detachment . . . but the Enemy did not come until the morning of the 24th when his Detachment was captured.[11]

It cannot be said for certain how the Secords learned of the American intention. Notwithstanding FitzGibbon's statement (written from memory 14 years after the event) that Mrs Secord's husband had learned of the plan, the Secord family tradition is that Mrs Secord overheard the conversation of some American officers who had come to her home and demanded a meal. Coincidental evidence suggests that one of those officers was Major Chapin. It was on 21 June that two of his men were captured by FitzGibbon on the Portage Road, after which, as Chapin said, he returned to Fort George and made his report to General Dearborn. His way to the fort led through Queenston. It may be deduced from Colonel Boerstler's "Narrative of the Expedition from Fort George to the Beaver Dams, U.C." that Major Chapin was a garrulous man. He visited Boerstler, talked of the ease with which FitzGibbon's post could be destroyed, and impressed Boerstler as "a vain, boasting liar".[12] Apparently Chapin was more persuasive with General Dearborn than with Boerstler, for the Baltimore inquiry revealed that it was upon intelligence derived from him that the expedition to Beaver Dams was planned.

After FitzGibbon received Mrs Secord's warning, he notified his superiors of the threatened attack and arranged with the Indians to intercept the American troops in the beechwoods. Early on the morning of 24 June, scouts reported to FitzGibbon that the enemy was advancing. He ordered out his detachment and went to reconnoitre. "I discovered him [the enemy] on the Mountain road, and took a position on an Eminence to the right of it", FitzGibbon said in his official report to Major De Haren.[13]

From his position he observed the progress of the battle. Around noon he noticed that the Indians were becoming tired, but he expected Major De Haren to arrive at any minute with reinforcements. FitzGibbon told James Somerville, in a letter written on the day of the battle, that "fearing that the Enemy would either drive me off or make his retreat good, I determined to come the old soldier over him and summon him to surrender".[14] FitzGibbon's ruse of threatening the Americans with a possible massacre by Indians whom he could not control may have been inspired by Brock's strategem at Detroit when he issued a similar warning to General Hull.

The consequences of the victory at Beaver Dams were various. On the American side, General Dearborn was removed from his post as commander in July 1813. Colonel Boerstler was severely criticized for surrendering his troops, but afterwards was exonerated by the inquiry held at Baltimore in 1815. The American army stayed on at Fort George in the summer of 1813, without attempting another attack until December, when it burned the village of Niagara and then retreated across the river to Fort Niagara.

Lieutenant James FitzGibbon became a national hero. A lengthy report in the *Montreal Gazette* of 6 July 1813 spoke of "the cool determination and the hardy presence of mind evinced by this highly meritorious officer in conducting the operations incident to the critical situation in which he was placed by his little band of heroes". FitzGibbon's fellow subalterns of the 49th Regiment presented him with a gold medal inscribed with a tribute to his daring exploit. Years later, Robert Baldwin, the politician, who was a boy of nine in 1813, told FitzGibbon that he never forgot the "boyish imagination and the pride which my young heart loved to feel in the consciousness that he whose praise was on every lip was the friend of my father's home".[15] But of greatest importance to the ambitious hero was the commendation of his superior officers. The adjutant-general, Major-General Edward Baynes, in a General Order of 28 June 1813, announced "a most judicious & spirited exploit achieved by a small Detachment of the 49th Regiment amounting to Forty-Six Rank and File under Lieut. FitzGibbon, and a band of Indian Warriors . . . "; while Lieutenant-General Sir George Prevost, commander-in-chief of the British forces in Canada, wrote a personal letter of congratulation to FitzGibbon in which he indicated his intention of "submitting the detail of your services, to His Royal Highness The Commander in Chief's favorable consideration".[16] A few months later, FitzGibbon received the reward that he desired — a captain's commission.

To the Indians, however, FitzGibbon was no hero. They felt bitterly resentful that while they had fought the battle, it was Lieutenant FitzGibbon who got the credit. Captain William Johnson Kerr, commander of the Six Nations at Beaver Dams, refused to let the matter drop, and in 1818 obtained a letter from FitzGibbon stating that

> With respect to the affair with Colonel Boerstler not a shot was fired on our side by any but the Indians. They beat the American Detachment into a state of terror and the only share I claim is the taking advantage of a favorable moment to offer them protection from the Tomahawk and the Scalping Knife. The Indian Department did all the rest.[17]

Why did FitzGibbon delay so long in giving the Indians the credit they deserved? The reason is clear. He wanted, above all, to win a captaincy, and for this, credit for the victory at Beaver Dams was essential. As he had said in his letter to Vincent a year previously, his success in the army henceforth would depend on his own exertions. His spectacular coup at Beaver Dams met the requirement perfectly. Privately he did praise the Indians. He said in his letter to Somerville, written after the battle, that the Indians had "hung close upon his [the enemy's] flank & rear and galled him severely", but he stopped short of saying that they had fought the entire battle. And with a shrewd eye towards publicity, FitzGibbon added a postscript to his letter: "Should you wish to give the public a sketch of these affairs pray draw up a summary in your own way". The glowing report that appeared in the *Montreal Gazette* of 6 July was the result.

The Indians were not alone in being deprived of recognition for their part in the victory at Beaver Dams.

FitzGibbon made no mention, either in his official report or in his letter to Somerville, of the advance warning he had received from Laura Secord. Accounts of her walk that were written in later years – the three certificates that FitzGibbon wrote for her, and Mrs Secord's own accounts in letters to government officials when asking for favours – were buried in government files. Her son Charles, in a letter that appeared in *The Church* (a periodical published in Cobourg, Ontario) on 18 April 1845, made the story public for the first time. Published with his letter was a copy of the certificate that FitzGibbon had written for Mrs Secord in 1837. Afterwards, Laura herself wrote a narrative that appeared in a Toronto journal, the *Anglo-American Magazine* of November 1853, as part of Gilbert Auchinleck's serial history of the War of 1812. A copy of the FitzGibbon certificate of 1837 accompanied the narrative.

These published accounts appeared to attract little attention. It was not until Laura Secord received a reward of £100 in gold from Albert Edward, Prince of Wales (the future King Edward VII), that her fame began to grow. The Prince sent her the gift after his Canadian tour of 1860, when he had visited Niagara Falls and had participated in a ceremony on Queenston Heights commemorating the death of Sir Isaac Brock. Mrs Secord, who was very determined as well as very courageous, had drawn the Prince of Wales' attention to her heroic deed by preparing a memorial to be presented to him on his tour. In her memorial, she described her service in the War of 1812, referred also to her deceased husband (he died in 1841) who had been wounded on Queenston Heights, and declared her loyalty to the Prince of Wales' mother, Queen Victoria. Attached to her memorial was a copy of James FitzGibbon's 1837 certificate. When Laura Secord received the royal reward, she was an old lady of 85.

Her celebrity as heroine was advanced further by a book that appeared in 1864. The author was William F. Coffin, a prominent government official and an early Canadian nationalist. In his book, *1812, the War and Its Moral*, Coffin gave an imaginative account of Laura's 33-kilometre walk from Queenston to Beaver Dams, telling how, in order to deceive the American sentry about the true purpose of her walk, she drove a cow before her until she reached the woods. The cow appealed to the popular imagination and the legend remains fixed in the minds of many Canadians. In fact, there is no evidence that Laura Secord's cow ever existed or that an American sentry stood in her path. Mrs. Secord died on 17 October 1868 at the age of 93, but her fame continued to grow for many years.

The question remains: why did James FitzGibbon neglect to mention Laura Secord's warning in his communications after the Battle of Beaver Dams? There are two explanations. First, as to his official report after the battle, which was addressed to Major De Haren, presumably De Haren had been notified earlier about Mrs Secord's message. The evidence for this is that Colonel Bisshopp, who had been stationed at Twenty Mile Creek, when reporting on the battle to General Vincent, expressed gratitude to Major De Haren "for his speedy movement to the point of attack and execution of the arrangements I had previously made with him".[18] Second, regarding the letter to James Somerville in which FitzGibbon described the events of the battle, it would have been very indiscreet for an officer like FitzGibbon to tell his friend about a secret message he had received. News of Mrs Secord's act of informing would have placed her and her family in grave danger as long as American troops were in the Niagara area.[19]

A year after the Battle of Beaver Dams, Captain FitzGibbon transferred to the Glengarry Light Infantry Fencibles, as there was no opening for a captain in his own 49th Regiment. The Fencibles had been recruited in British North America specifically and exclusively to meet the threat of American invasion. While they were attached to the British army like the regular regiments, they were not expected to serve outside North America. FitzGibbon did not foresee that at the war's end the Fencibles would become dispensable.

As leader of the partisans and at Beaver Dams, James FitzGibbon had shown that he was courageous, daring, quick-witted, skilful in deception, even wily, as Major Cyrenius Chapin said of him later. These characteristics suited him for reconnaissance, and it was mainly in that capacity that he served in the last year of the war. His last action in battle was at Lundy's Lane in July 1814 when the Glengarry Fencibles held the British right wing. Although this was the bloodiest battle of the war, Captain FitzGibbon emerged without a scratch. Afterwards, he did some reconnaissance for Lieutenant-General Gordon Drummond at Fort Erie, and for a time served as commander of the Battalion of Incorporated Militia. But the end of the war was now imminent. It came with the signing of the Treaty of Ghent on Christmas Eve, 1814.

FitzGibbon hated to admit to himself that his military career was over. He tried to obtain another promotion by addressing a memorial to the commander-in-chief, His Royal Highness, the Duke of York, asking for the brevet rank of major. The promotion was denied. The Glengarry Light Infantry Fencibles were disbanded in early summer, 1816, and Captain James FitzGibbon was retired on half pay. Before that happened, however, he had faced up to the reality that confronted him, and had accepted a position in the public service of Upper Canada.

Chapter Four

First Step in the Public Service: the Militia Office

On the first of June 1816, James FitzGibbon became a clerk in the office of the adjutant-general of militia, Upper Canada. It was a position that carried little prestige; indeed, it must have been humiliating for an army captain to accept so lowly a post. The salary was less than FitzGibbon had received as captain — 7s. 6d. provincial currency per day, compared with 11s. 7d. sterling in the army (provincial currency being worth ten percent less than sterling). Fortunately, his retired captain's half pay raised his total income above what it had been in the army.

In accepting his clerical post, James FitzGibbon had little choice. There were few employment opportunities in Upper Canada, and he had few qualifications. Apart from his military training, he had had no experience except tenant farming in Ireland. As a war veteran and retired captain, he was entitled to a land grant of 800 acres, but he did not receive the grant until 1817. Even if he had wished to farm, he had no capital with which to buy livestock and equipment. What he did have was a friend in the government service.

In Upper Canada the path to success lay through government patronage. FitzGibbon's friend was the adjutant-general of militia, Lieutenant-Colonel Nathaniel

Coffin, who had served as provincial aide-de-camp to Major-General Sir Roger Hale Sheaffe (his cousin and brother-in-law) when the latter acted as commander-in-chief and administrator of the province following the death of Brock. When it was announced early in 1816 that the Glengarry Fencibles were to be disbanded, Colonel Coffin called on Captain FitzGibbon and asked him to accept the post of clerk in his department. James did not hesitate long. He had a wife and baby girl to support, and he was badly in debt. Far from paying off the sum of £150 owed since his first commission, he had gone more deeply into debt during the war. He had considered it necessary, for instance, to have a horse when he led the partisans, though he received no allowance for one.

James' marriage took place in 1814. Little is known about his wife, Mary Haley, except that she and James had been friends since he had been stationed in Quebec in the early 1800s. At that time, when Mary was a young girl, James gave her a book, *The Beauties of Hervey*, which is now in the possession of a descendant. The inscription, in FitzGibbon's handwriting, reads, "To Miss Mary Haley from a Friend". In a youthful hand, probably Mary's, are the words, "Mr. J. FitzGibbon, 49th Regt., Quebec". At the time of their marriage, Mary was 21 or 22. James was 33.

The wedding ceremony was performed in the Anglican Church, Adolphustown, by the Reverend George Okill Stuart of Kingston, on 14 August 1814. FitzGibbon rode on horseback from Fort Erie to Adolphustown, (about 325 kilometres), on a three-day leave, for the wedding. He met Mary at the church and parted from her immediately after the ceremony, as he had to hurry back to Fort Erie. He explained to Anna Brownell Jameson when she visited Canada some years later, that "there was a little girl that I loved, and I knew that if I could but marry her before I was killed, and I a captain, she would have the pension of a captain's widow".[1] Evidently, Mary Haley was not from a rich family. Was she, perhaps, the daughter of an Irish soldier, possibly killed in the war? Her family background remains a mystery. Even FitzGibbon's granddaughter, Mary Agnes FitzGibbon, in describing the "romantic" marriage of her grandfather in

A Veteran of 1812, the Life of James FitzGibbon, offers no information.

James and Mary FitzGibbon, with baby daughter Mary, took up residence in Fort York, three kilometres west of the small provincial capital of York (population around 800). Their dwelling was the four-room apartment that had been provided for the adjutant-general of militia, quarters erected when the fort was rebuilt after its destruction by the Americans in 1813. The promise of free accommodation was probably one of the inducements that Colonel Coffin offered when urging FitzGibbon to become the militia clerk. This was the only award attached to the position. Unlike many posts in Upper Canada, this one carried no fees. James was approaching middle age, but he was adaptable, with an agile mind and a keen sense of humour – qualities that helped him adjust to the routine of the militia office. The work must have seemed agonizingly dull after the excitement of a partisan's life, of winning the surrender of an army by one's wits, even of serving as a reconnaissance officer.

When FitzGibbon joined the adjutant-general's office, the militia consisted of some 30 regiments and about 14,000 officers and men. In the next ten years, the number of regiments increased to 54 and the number of militiamen more than doubled. The militia had emerged from the War of 1812 with a record of valiant service. Granted that the brunt of the fighting had fallen on the regular troops and the fencibles, nevertheless the militia, and especially the Battalion of Incorporated Militia, had performed well its essential task of supplementing the regulars when and where needed. According to law, every able-bodied man between the ages of 16 and 60 was required to enroll in the militia, but training was negligible. The commanding officer of each militia regiment was expected to call out his regiment from two to four times a year for inspection and instruction. Once a year, on the King's birthday, a review or muster of all the regiments was held, after which the commanding officers were ordered by law to transmit muster rolls of their respective companies. The commanding officers often neglected to send in these reports, which the adjutant-general required for his annual report. The militia clerk soon

Fort York, FitzGibbon's workplace and residence while clerk in the adjutant-general's office

found that one of his most repetitious and undoubtedly irritating duties was to send reminders to the militia officers about their overdue muster rolls. Even more tedious was the responsibility of maintaining the records of correspondence and militia general orders. These he copied by hand in huge volumes of correspondence and general orders which may be seen in the Public Archives of Canada today. They show that FitzGibbon, bored or not, performed the task conscientiously and well. No doubt he preferred writing letters to copying those of others and he had a fair amount of correspondence to do. Many of the letters, such as the reminders about muster rolls, were of a routine nature; others dealt with war claims, officers' commissions, and so on.

The Board of Militia Claims had been set up to investigate the claims of militia veterans for back pay, lodging money, forage charges and bounties for recruits owing since the War of 1812. Adjutant-General Coffin served on the board, and all claims were processed through his office, as were claims for pensions available to disabled militiamen and the widows of militiamen who had died in the war. All these claims had to be justified by certificates from the appropriate officers verifying the service performed by the claimant or the claimant's late husband. While FitzGibbon conducted most of the correspondence involved, the actual payments were made by the paymaster of militia claims, William Allan, who was appointed to that post in 1818.

As the Upper Canada militia increased in size, so did the number of requests for promotions and officers' commissions, all of which required appropriate documentation. Colonel Coffin reported to Lieutenant-Governor Maitland in 1818 "that 500 Commissions for the Militia have been prepared and issued from the Adjutant General's office within two years and a half, and that there are upwards of 100 Commissions at this moment wanted in the different Regiments in this Province".[2] Every commission had to be approved by the lieutenant-governor, who was officially head of the militia. His approval was required as well for promotions or resignations of militia officers, and for the formation of new regiments, indeed for all militia decisions of any consequence whatsoever.

These matters were routed through the adjutant-general's office, thus leading to frequent consultations between the adjutant-general and the lieutenant-governor or his private secretary. Colonel Coffin was frequently away from the office. He accompanied Lieutenant-Governor Francis Gore to Amherstburg and Quebec in 1816, for example, and two years later spent six months in Quebec while serving on the Board of Militia Claims. During the Maitland régime, he often went with the lieutenant-governor to the latter's elegant 22-room "cottage" on the Stamford Park estate near Niagara, where Sir Peregrine Maitland and his wife (daughter of the Duke of Richmond) habitually spent weeks or months. During such absences FitzGibbon took charge of the office. He soon developed his own friendly relations with the staff in the lieutenant-governor's office and eventually with the lieutenant-governor himself, who, as FitzGibbon well knew, was the ultimate source of all patronage.

After three years in the militia office, FitzGibbon became discontented with his lot. It was not just the increased pressure of his work. He was disturbed by the irregularity in payment of his salary. A lapse occurred when the Honourable Samuel Smith, provincial administrator for the period between the departure of Lieutenant-Governor Gore in 1817 and the arrival of Sir Peregrine Maitland in 1818, refused to sign the necessary warrant. The clerk's salary had previously been paid from the contingent expense allowance of the adjutant-general, but the act that established the fund did not provide authorization for such payment. In fact, the position of clerk in the militia office had never been officially established.

This anomalous situation had come about as follows. Colonel Coffin had been appointed deputy adjutant-general of militia in January 1814, while the ailing Aeneas Shaw continued as adjutant-general. Shaw died the following March. Coffin continued as deputy to the next adjutant-general, Lieutenant-Colonel C.L.L. Foster, until the latter was transferred to Lower Canada. Coffin was promoted in March 1815 to adjutant-general, and the deputy's post disappeared. Coffin had to carry on the work formerly done by two men. The Legislature in its 1816 session authorized an increased expenditure of £165 for the office but did not specify the precise use to be made of the additional funds. No mention was made of a clerk. Coffin adopted the practice of paying FitzGibbon's salary from the allowance for contingent expenses, a practice that Lieutenant-Governor Gore supported by sending regular letters of authorization for the clerk's pay to the adjutant-general. At first, Smith went along with the practice, but in the summer of 1818 refused, saying it was not legal under the act. Although Maitland regularized the situation after his arrival in August 1818, FitzGibbon, under financial burdens, resigned from the militia office early in 1819 to become a private land agent. His daughter Mary now had two brothers, Charles Thomas, born in 1817, and George, born in 1818. (A third boy, William Wilder, was born in October 1819). James found that he could not support his growing family on his clerk's salary and he believed that he could earn more as a land agent.

FitzGibbon embarked on his new venture in partnership with a fellow Irishman, Benjamin Geale, who like himself had a military background (former lieutenant in the 41st Regiment) and who had been a government clerk in Lieutenant-Governor Gore's office. An advertisement appeared in the *Upper Canada Gazette* early in April 1819, announcing that B. Geale and J. FitzGibbon had established a general land agency office in York, Upper Canada. "Emigrants, and all others applying for Lands from the Crown, can obtain every requisite assistance and information", the advertisement stated, declaring further that "This Office will afford the easiest and most profitable means of enabling Persons to purchase or sell Lands in any part of the Province". The partners also provided the essential service of administering the Oath of Allegiance, without which no one could obtain land in Upper Canada. At first, only Geale was qualified to administer the oath, but in April 1821, FitzGibbon obtained his commission to do so in the Home District.

Many settlers were coming into the province in those postwar years, and the land agency of Geale and FitzGibbon flourished. They located nearly 500 settlers in their first nine months of operations. FitzGibbon's hope for an increase in income was realized. In his first two years as land agent, he earned £250 per year, compared with his clerk's salary of £137 16s. 6d. Yet he gave up this advantageous enterprise and in May 1821 returned to the adjutant-general's office. Why? The explanation he offered, years later, was that Colonel Coffin urged him to return to the office, and that he agreed to do so "if he [Coffin] procured for me ten Shillings Sterling per day, being the allowance made to the first Clerk in each of the other Departments of the Government. And this offer I made because I desired to serve the Government if I could obtain even nearly the income required to Support my Family".[3] Coffin presented the case to Lieutenant-Governor Maitland with the result that an order-in-council was passed providing for a clerk in the adjutant-general's office at the yearly salary of £202 currency (£182 sterling). In addition, Coffin agreed that FitzGibbon might administer the Oath of Allegiance in his office, as he had recently been doing as land agent. Such a commission was worth around £75 per year in fees, and would therefore bring FitzGibbon's income above what he had been earning in his agency.

James FitzGibbon's alleged desire to serve the government had a noble ring to it, but it is likely that at the time he made his decision to return to the militia office, other considerations were uppermost in his mind. For one thing, his partner Benjamin Geale had become seriously ill. (He died in 1821). Geale was appointed master-in-chancery of the Legislative Council in 1820. Obviously, the burden of the land agency was falling increasingly on FitzGibbon's shoulders. At the same time, FitzGibbon was becoming more and more involved in governmental affairs, and must have had little time left for his business. Moreover, the desire for the greater security of a government post was probably strong. His family increased to five in March 1821 when his fourth son, James Gerald, was born. But perhaps most important of all, this astute Irishman, with his shrewdness and foresight, must have envisioned the possibility of profiting from the patronage system. With this in mind, what better place to be than in an office that worked closely with that of the lieutenant-governor? Especially when that official, Sir Peregrine Maitland, was showing signs of favouring him.

The first indication that Maitland was taking a special interest in FitzGibbon came in the form of a commission as lieutenant-colonel in the militia, commanding the Third (afterwards the West) York Regiment of Militia. That was in January 1820. Two months later, Maitland made FitzGibbon a justice of the peace, Home District, an appointment that was renewed in the future many times. This was followed by an assignment from January to May 1821 as assistant to the clerk in the Executive Council office. Next came the commission to administer the Oath of Allegiance, and then the order-in-council enabling FitzGibbon to return as clerk in the militia office on his own terms.

The key to the puzzle as to why the distinguished aloof aristocrat, Sir Peregine Maitland, should single out for favouritism an obscure land agent, formerly a militia clerk, and a retired captain on half pay, is found in one word, "Brock". Maitland was a major-general and a bemedalled veteran of the Napoleonic wars. He had commanded the First Brigade of Guards in the Battle of Waterloo, and was rewarded afterwards with a medal (his third) and a knighthood (K.C.B.). It is not known whether Maitland and Sir Isaac Brock had ever met (Brock was eight years older than Maitland and had belonged to a different regiment) but there was the common bond of military service during the crucial Napoleonic era.

It was Sir Isaac's brother, John Savery, who drew Maitland's attention to James FitzGibbon. This he did by writing to Maitland before the latter left England to take up his post as lieutenant-governor of Upper Canada. In his letter, Brock requested Maitland to "kindly notice Captain FitzGibbon, now a half-pay officer settled at York". Beginning as a sergeant in the 49th Regiment, Brock said, FitzGibbon had "by his zeal in his profession, attracted the notice of my late brother Sir Isaac, who recommended him for a commission to His Royal Highness the Commander in Chief". Brock went on to tell how FitzGibbon, in the War of 1812, had "by his presence of mind caused a large body of Americans to surrender to his handful of men". He concluded his letter with these words:

Sir Peregrine Maitland, Lieutenant-Governor of Upper Canada, 1818-1828

> Should you, Sir, ever have occasion for the services of Captain FitzGibbon you will find in him a faithful and grateful officer; and any favor you will be pleased to shew him, independently of his own merits, from the knowledge he was a favorite and protegé of my late brother, will ever be thankfully acknowledged by . . . John Savery Brock.[4]

Maitland continued to show his partiality towards FitzGibbon as long as he remained lieutenant-governor of Upper Canada, and his partiality was not limited to appointments and commissions. For the celebration of the King's birthday, 23 April 1822, Maitland chose Lieutenant-Colonel FitzGibbon to command the guard of honour, on the grounds that FitzGibbon had commanded the Battalion of Incorporated Militia for a time on the Niagara frontier. Members of the East and West Regiments of York Militia, together with the troop of cavalry attached to the North York Regiment, formed the guard of honour in front of Government House to receive the colours, "which his Majesty had been graciously pleased to command should be prepared" and which were inscribed "Niagara" in commemoration of the services rendered there by the Incorporated Militia. Lieutenant-Governor Maitland, as the King's representative, presented the colours, and the guard of honour then marched "with Band playing and Colors flying" to place the colours at Government House.[5]

Meanwhile, FitzGibbon had resumed his duties in the militia office. There he found that the pressure of militia claims for back pay and pensions had subsided, but now, claims for land grants were inundating the office. These claims were the result of an order-in-council of January 1820 that authorized land grants for militia veterans of the War of 1812. In the next two years, nearly 3,000 certificates for land grants were issued from the militia office, each one preceded by an examination of the applicant's record. In the midst of all this paperwork, friction developed between Colonel Coffin and his clerk.

Although Colonel Coffin had appeared eager to have FitzGibbon return to work for him, he soon reneged on his promise to let his clerk administer the Oath of Allegiance in the militia office. The adjutant-general was facing a serious financial problem. His salary of £365 per year had been sharply reduced when the act, granting part of his salary, had expired in March 1820. Coffin was anxious to persuade the House of Assembly to restore the full amount, but he knew that some Assembly members objected to voting more money for him while his clerk, they said, spent much of his time administering the Oath of Allegiance. (FitzGibbon later denied this accusation, claiming that he worked before and after office hours to make up for lost time). In order to get the goodwill of the Assembly, Coffin prevailed upon Lieutenant-Governor Maitland not to renew FitzGibbon's commission to administer the oath. This appeasing step worked. In March 1823, the Legislature passed an act that made permanent provision for the adjutant-general's salary of £365 per annum. At the same time, the act established the new position of assistant adjutant-general of militia with a yearly salary of £150, provincial currency. "Thus did the Government sanction an Act", FitzGibbon wrote, "by which I was deprived of £52 15s. 6d. per annum, while at the same time I was taken from my obscurity and raised to the rank of Assistant Adjutant-General".[6] The Assembly made partial amends later by granting FitzGibbon an additional £50 per annum.

Annoyed though he was by his salary reduction, FitzGibbon observed the courtesy of writing to thank Maitland for his new appointment. His letter was ingratiating:

> Permit me to offer to Your Excellency a very humble tribute of unfeigned gratitude for the Appointment you have been pleased to bestow upon me.
>
> This and other appointments with which your Excellency has before honored me, have to me a peculiar value. Twenty four years ago I left my Father's house a Serjeant in one of His Majesty's Regiments; his last words expressed an entire confidence that I would ever conduct myself agreeably to the lessons which he had so carefully taught me. Both my Parents are, I trust, still living and will again be blessed in witnessing how the almighty continues to reward them for their earnest though humble efforts to instruct their Children.
>
> I feel confident that this short Statement will not

> be unfavourably received, nor deemed impertinent by Your Excellency; nor if I add that there are others who have been pleased to take a warm interest in my welfare, and to whom my advancement will be highly gratifying.[7]

His Excellency gave no indication of finding FitzGibbon's letter "impertinent", and it would not be long before he would show his trust in FitzGibbon by asking him to carry out an important assignment.

At the time FitzGibbon wrote his letter to Maitland, he had lived in York seven years and had become a familiar figure to the citizens of that growing town (population now around 1,400). He was in his early forties, and was distinguished by "his tall, muscular figure, ever in buoyant motion; his grey, good humoured, vivacious eye beaming out from underneath a bushy, light-coloured eyebrow; the cheery ring of his voice and its animated utterances were familiar to everyone". This description was written some years later from personal memory by the Reverend Henry Scadding, FitzGibbon's junior by 30 years. Scadding noted also that the colonel was one of the "remarkable group . . . that assembled habitually in the church at York".[8] The church was, of course, St James Anglican, which was presided over by the Reverend (afterwards Bishop) John Strachan, and which had a canopied pew reserved for the lieutenant-governor. St James was the right church for ambitious people in York to attend. FitzGibbon had purchased a pew as early as January 1818.

He had formed other connections as well. He had become a prominent Mason. His rise in that society may have carried little weight in government circles but it gave FitzGibbon an acquaintance with a wide range of people, which proved to be of some significance in the disturbing days prior to the outbreak of rebellion in 1837. FitzGibbon first joined the Order of Freemasonry in Quebec when he was stationed there shortly after his arrival in Canada. After he moved to York, he became affiliated with St Andrews Lodge, no. 1.

In the Order of Freemasonry, James FitzGibbon was accepted on his personal merits without regard to his education, family background or lack of wealth. Proof of this came when he was elected in 1822 to the highest Masonic office possible in Upper Canada, that of deputy provincial grand master. The top office, provincial grand master, was held in England, according to the colonial custom of the time. As deputy grand master, Brother FitzGibbon took an unorthodox approach. When he addressed the meeting of the Provincial Grand Lodge at York in 1823, his address resembled a sermon on love, justice and education rather than the customary report on matters relating to the Masonic Order. The intricacies of Masonic procedure and craft were not what concerned FitzGibbon. He was more interested in the Order's potential for teaching harmony and brotherly love, especially among the people of Upper Canada. In his address as deputy grand master, he struck a modern note, pleading for tolerance and better education:

> Our population being made up of persons of many nations, languages and religions, need we wonder at sometimes hearing the offensive terms of insolent Englishmen! selfish Scot! savage Irishman! cunning Yankee! And do we not all know most valuable characters of these several nations? . . .
>
> I hope I shall live to see the day when this fraternity will be found, proceeding upon a well organized system, to give effect to schools already established; to establish new ones whenever and wherever wanted; to the formation of libraries in every town and township; proceeding, in short, to make war upon ignorance, which is of all evils the greatest enemy of man, with a skill and energy deserving of success.[9]

These were not empty words. In the coming years, FitzGibbon demonstrated his belief in tolerance by striving to improve relations between Roman Catholics and members of the militant Protestant Orange Association. He gave proof of his interest in education by becoming a founding member, in 1830, of the York Mechanics' Institute, an adult education society that eventually formed the basis of the Toronto Public Library. And he became an active supporter of Upper Canada College, the school established by Lieutenant-Governor Colborne.

As deputy provincial grand master, FitzGibbon was irritated at having to get approval for all decisions from the grand master of the Masons in England and, on occasion, he overstepped his authority in issuing dispensations to lodges. He found, moreover, that the increasing pressure of work in the public service left him little time for his Masonic responsibilities, and after three years he resigned from his high office.

FitzGibbon had held his post of assistant adjutant-general of militia about a year, when Lieutenant-Governor Maitland gave him the important assignment mentioned previously. This was to investigate the causes of rioting that had occurred among the settlers of Ramsay township of the Bathurst District, in the northeastern part of the province. Two groups of immigrants were involved – the Irish, brought out by Peter Robinson in the fall of 1823, and the settlers who had come out a few years earlier. The situation had become aggravated when the magistrates of the district had attempted to restore order, and an Irish settler had been killed. Alarmed by the tense situation, the magistrates asked the lieutenant-governor to send a detachment of regular troops to be stationed in the neighbourhood until peace and order could be restored. The magistrates referred to the Irish as "a set of lawless banditti [who] were threatening destruction to the lives and property of every honest individual".[10] Maitland refused to send troops, promising only that the military detachment stationed at Kingston would be held in readiness to march to Perth if the need arose. Instead of troops, as FitzGibbon said, "His Excellency was pleased to send me alone, speaking the Gaelic language as I did, and being favourably known to my Countrymen".[11]

This assignment was different from anything that FitzGibbon had done before, and he agreed with reluctance to accept it. He had just attended the burial of his recently-born child, and his wife was suffering from grief and poor health. The journey to Perth was not an easy one. The first part, from York to Kingston, was a pleasant enough voyage on Lake Ontario by steamboat, but the final 80 kilometres from Kingston to Perth had to be made over a very rough road by horse-and-wagon or on horseback. He arrived at Perth on 18 May 1824.

He faced a delicate and formidable task. Tensions between the recent Irish immigrants, who were mainly

Catholic, and the earlier Protestant settlers, who were chiefly Scottish but included some Irish, had led to the rioting. The fighting had begun on the day of the annual militia muster, the King's birthday, 23 April, when the militiamen had gathered after the muster in Alexander Morris' "groggery" at Morphy's Falls (Carleton Place). The Irish were out-slugged in the fight but got their revenge by returning to the tavern twice over the weekend, breaking into it and destroying the property within. A few days later, the sheriff, J.H. Powell, and the magistrates of the district, decided to take the law into their own hands. They organized a party led by the deputy sheriff, which went from Perth to the immigrants' temporary settlement at Shepherd's Falls (Almonte). A number of them then proceeded to Cornelius Roche's log house and blacksmith shop, known to be a popular meeting place of the Irish. Shots were fired, killing one of the Irish and wounding two others.

There can be little doubt that FitzGibbon's sympathies lay with the recent Irish settlers whose background he understood so well, but he tried to be objective, and began his investigations by obtaining the cooperation of the magistrates. They appointed Magistrate Benjamin Delisle to accompany him. FitzGibbon stayed in the district three weeks, going about the settlements, talking to old and new immigrants, asking questions, taking sworn statements and, as he said, "reasoning with both parties, and soothing the irritated feelings of all".[12] While waiting in Kingston for the boat to take him back to York on 10 June, FitzGibbon prepared a perceptive report for the lieutenant-governor.

The primary cause of the trouble, he stated, was a feeling of jealousy on the part of the old settlers who thought that Robinson's Irish settlers had "received more of the Bounty of Government" than they had. (The government *had* been more generous with the later settlers). Religious and party distinctions had added to the ill feeling. Secondly, Peter Robinson had left a young man, Thomas Baines, in charge of the immigrant depot at Shepherd's Falls, and Baines, according to FitzGibbon, lacked "that respectability of character peculiar to maturity and experience, neither was he invested with any

Official Authority in the District". (A few years later, Baines became secretary of the Upper Canada Clergy Corporation and was thus responsible for collecting rents and performing other duties in connection with the clergy reserves). FitzGibbon found fault with the militia officers for giving liquor to the militiamen on the day of the muster, which was against the law, and he detected "a want of cordiality" between the magistrates and the sheriff, because of which "proper preventative measures were not taken to ensure the execution of the law". In particular, FitzGibbon deplored "the selecting, organizing and arming of the party" under the deputy sheriff, Alexander Matheson, who was "a man of overbearing and insolent conduct, and an Orange man whose father it is said was murdered by the Catholics in Ireland; all who spoke of the selection in my hearing described it as a very partial one, because too many Orange men were chosen". FitzGibbon even suggested that "all the deeds of violence" were committed by Orangemen. He stated that the firing on the people inside the blacksmith's house had been done by the deputy sheriff's party although no shots had been fired by those inside. He based this conclusion on a careful examination of the bullet holes in the log house and of the pistol supposedly used in the shooting by someone inside the house. In sum, FitzGibbon considered the conduct of the deputy sheriff's party "a wanton and outrageous attack upon the lives of the new settlers" not only in the shooting at Roche's house but also by others of the party who had pursued some of the settlers from their huts to the river, firing as they went. FitzGibbon did not report on the conduct of the Irish settlers in the fracas at Morris' tavern, because the magistrates had already taken affidavits, arrests had been made, and the accused would be tried in the courts.[13]

While FitzGibbon condemned the officers of the law in his report, and accused the Orangemen of resorting to violence, he privately offered advice to the Irish, who were considering bringing legal action for false imprisonment against those who had made arrests. In a letter to Thomas Baines, FitzGibbon urged forebearance: "Let this Season be employed by them [the Irish] to sow seed from which the food for their Families may be obtained, instead of sowing the seeds of hatred and revenge which ever abundantly produce poverty and crime". He reminded Baines that the people in the deputy sheriff's party had believed that they were doing their duty and that they too were poor. "Let these poor people therefore be left in peace with their Families, and let the Irishmen be the first to show the spirit of foregiveness, and to set the example, common alike to good Catholics and to good Protestants, of obeying the blessed commandment of the Saviour of both, in doing to others as they wish others would do to them". FitzGibbon asked Baines to read his letter to the Irish settlers and to use his influence towards acceptance of its message.[14]

There was no more rioting among the settlers of Bathurst District. In the August assizes at Perth, some of the sheriff's men were prosecuted for firing on the immigrants' camp but were acquitted for lack of evidence; four of the Irish settlers were convicted for rioting, fined £10 and sentenced to two months' imprisonment. The deputy sheriff, perhaps due to his position in the community, was not prosecuted. The settlers of Ramsay township continued to pursue their occupation of tilling the soil and laying the foundation of a productive and peaceful community. An unexpected result was that FitzGibbon's talent as mediator was revealed, and he was called upon to use this ability in future crises.

Sir Peregrine Maitland had his own reasons to be pleased with the outcome of FitzGibbon's investigation of the riots. Not only had peace been restored, but FitzGibbon's report helped the lieutenant-governor to win a dispute with Lord Dalhousie, the governor-in-chief of Canada. The two governors disagreed about immigration policy. Maitland wanted to bring more Irish immigrants to Upper Canada, but Dalhousie opposed the plan. He wrote to the colonial secretary, Lord Bathurst, in May, saying that "After what has now occurred [in Ramsay township], the peaceable and industrious settlers in these woods will never be reconciled to their Irish neighbours, even in small numbers". Later in the summer, Maitland, armed with FitzGibbon's report, which he enclosed in a letter to Lord Bathurst, wrote that "All is now quiet". The magistrates, he said, had "over-rated the danger . . . .

The report of the Assistant Adjutant General of Militia and the present quiet conduct of the emigrants confirm the view of things which I had taken".[15]

With this assurance, Lord Bathurst instructed Peter Robinson to proceed with a second movement of immigrants from the south of Ireland. These immigrants, numbering about 2,000, came to Upper Canada the following year. Most settled in the Newcastle District (Peterborough county). This movement led to the first encounter between James FitzGibbon and William Lyon Mackenzie, the contentious editor of the *Colonial Advocate.*

Mackenzie had emigrated from Scotland in 1820, at the age of 25, and four years later founded his newspaper in Queenston. In his very first issue of 18 May 1824, he attacked the lieutenant-governor, "a right valiant and most excellent military chieftain . . . a knight of noble birth and noble connexions" who, Mackenzie said, enjoyed himself "like the country he governs, in inactivity – whose migrations are, by water, from York to Queenston, and from Queenston to York [16] . . . who knows our wants as he gains a knowledge of the time of day, by *report* . . ." Members of the inner circle of government, such as Attorney-General John Beverley Robinson, viewed the editor as a troublemaker, a new version of that other Scottish troublemaker, Robert Gourlay. In the fall of 1824, Mackenzie moved to York where he would be closer to the scene of political action.

Mackenzie turned his attention to the Irish immigrants of the Newcastle District. In an editorial comment headed "Mr. Robinson's Irish Settlers", he claimed to have information "that these people have an ardent desire to go to the United States, and that they frequently desert. No less than thirty of them decamped lately in one night". This item, which appeared in the *Colonial Advocate* of 8 December 1825, seemed to confirm the rumours about defections of the Irish immigrants to the United States, especially while they were encamped at Kingston and Cobourg waiting for transportation to their settlements. By the time the item appeared, however, the immigrants had moved to their new homes.

FitzGibbon was angered by the charge that the Irish were defectors and, by implication, poor settlers. While on a trip to Cobourg to attend a militia court martial, he took the opportunity to visit the new settlements. Afterwards he wrote a letter to the *Quebec Mercury* and other newspapers protesting against Mackenzie's accusation and declaring that only one family (who had relatives in the United States) had actually gone there to live. Almost all the Irish, he said, had settled on their land. In response to FitzGibbon's published letter, Mackenzie defended himself in his newspaper, saying that reports on immigration defections were contradictory, but that he would be glad to supply FitzGibbon with the name of the person from whom he had received his original information. Colonel FitzGibbon immediately challenged the informant to declare himself and reveal the evidence on which he had based his charge. The informant turned out to be a prominent citizen of Cobourg, Zaccheus Burnham, treasurer of Newcastle District, survey contractor of new townships in the district, and a member of the House of Assembly. Burnham wrote to FitzGibbon saying that he had met Mackenzie on the steamboat going from York to Niagara, that Mackenzie had asked him about his recent visit to the Irish settlements and that he had replied: "It was said some of them while at Cobourg took passage in a schooner for Rochester". On being asked by Mackenzie how many, "I said thirty persons", but added that "I only spoke from hearsay". Burnham concluded his letter with the statement, "I believe the settlers generally are contented".[17] And so FitzGibbon had the satisfaction of tracking down a harmful rumour, exposing its shaky foundation, and vindicating his own faith in the Irish settlers.

The antagonism that this controversy aroused between FitzGibbon and Mackenzie reached its climax in the battle at Montgomery's Tavern in 1837. There was a certain similarity in their backgrounds. Both had grown up in "the old country", one in Ireland, and the other in Scotland, and both had suffered from poverty in childhood. But they had chosen paths of different directions. FitzGibbon had adopted a military career, and although he had not attained a very high rung in the military hierarchy, he never lost his respect for those in authority. Unlike Mackenzie, he was neither a rebel nor a politician. He admired Sir Peregrine Maitland for his proven ability as a military commander and respected him as the King's representative. Mackenzie, on his part, liked nothing better than to puncture the pretentious balloons of pompous officials. With his fierce Scottish independence, the little red-wigged editor would bow to no man, least of all to an English officer and aristocrat like Lieutenant-Governor Maitland.

Mackenzie had not yet become active in politics. His newspaper, the *Colonial Advocate*, was a mixed bag of news items from far and near, reports of Parliamentary debates, biting editorial comment, and advertisements galore. He had a bent for malicious gossip, and in the summer of 1826 published a series of imaginary discussions led by a fictional Patrick Swift, said to be the nephew of the Irish satirist Jonathan Swift. In the discussions, scurrilous things were said of leading members of the governing clique: J.B. Robinson, Rev. John Strachan, William Allan, and others. These attacks might well have been the last gasps of a newspaper on the verge of financial collapse had it not been for the foolish antics of some young men close to the group known as the Family Compact. On 8 June 1826 these rowdies broke into the printing plant of the *Colonial Advocate*, destroyed the press and scattered the type. The perpetrators bore prominent names such as Baby, Jarvis and Sherwood. One of them, John Lyons, was a clerk in the lieutenant-governor's office. Within a few weeks of the outrage, Maitland dismissed Lyons from his office. (But a year later, Lyons was appointed registrar of the counties of Lincoln and Haldimand). All the offenders were brought to trial in the fall and found guilty. Mackenzie was awarded damages of £625, sufficient to enable him to buy a new and better press, and to revive his newspaper.

Up to the time of the trial, FitzGibbon had stayed out of the affair, but the fine levied on the young men spurred him to action. J.C. Dent, Toronto journalist and historian of the Upper Canadian Rebellion, described FitzGibbon as "rash, impetuous and indiscreet", words that suited perfectly FitzGibbon's act of soliciting donations to help the press rioters pay their fine. This step led to the charge in the radical newspaper, the *Canadian Freeman*, that several heads of government departments and the lieutenant-governor himself had contributed to the fund for the rioters. FitzGibbon, never able to resist rushing into print to defend himself, wrote a letter to the editor, Francis Collins, declaring that the assertion was untrue "so far as the Lieutenant-Governor was concerned", thus seeming to confirm the first part of the charge. Exactly who the contributors were remained a mystery. FitzGibbon burned the list of names, according to Dent.[18]

Some time later, when FitzGibbon became afraid that his indiscretion might react unfavourably on his career, he prepared a statement for the lieutenant-governor, outlining the reasons for his action. Putting the best possible face on it, he said that although he regretted "the injury to property which took place", he could not "overlook the scandalous conduct" of the owner, Mackenzie, which "drove the Individuals concerned to Commit the trespass". He considered also that the entire community had been insulted by the newspaper and therefore the young men should not have to bear the full burden of the damages charged against them. For these reasons, he said, he had solicited donations from sympathetic persons, asking the donors to send the money to the attorney who was acting for the young men. FitzGibbon stated that he did not know the precise amount that had been contributed but he believed that it was less than £400. Finally, FitzGibbon declared that, having no connection by relationship or otherwise with the young men, he had felt that in canvassing for the donations he could not be accused of selfishness.[19]

When James FitzGibbon made this statement, he was no longer employed in the militia office. Lieutenant-Governor Maitland had promoted him to the House of Assembly as its clerk, in May 1827. Fear for his future career, sparked by a rumour that the Assembly intended to question his conduct in canvassing on behalf of the law offenders, prompted him to offer his explanation. His fear proved groundless. Nevertheless his promotion was widely interpreted as a reward for his special services to those offenders, belonging as they did to prominent families. Undoubtedly the appointment confirmed Maitland's favouritism towards FitzGibbon, but whether it came as a reward for that particular service is not certain. It was one step in the sequence of appointments and distinctions that the lieutenant-governor conferred upon him. One of these, his commission as a full colonel in the militia, which he received prior to the affair of Mackenzie's printing press, fitted more closely the pattern of a reward – a reward for FitzGibbon's success in carrying out the lieutenant-governor's mission among the fighting settlers of the Bathurst District.

Chapter Five

A Plurality of Offices

The new clerk of the House of Assembly replaced an officer who had held the post for 14 years. Maitland transferred the former clerk, Dr Grant Powell, to the Legislative Council as its clerk, a position of greater prestige but with no increase in salary. Powell, a former surgeon with the Incoroprated Militia, belonged to a distinguished Upper Canadian family. His father, William Dummer Powell, had been for nine years chief justice of Upper Canada and speaker of the Legislative Council. He was a man of authority, prestige and influence. Grant, his third son, had as benefactor Sir Roger Hale Sheaffe while the latter served his brief term as administrator of Upper Canada. Sheaffe bestowed on Grant Powell two appointments in one year (1813), those of Assembly clerk and official principal of the Court of Probate. Sir Peregrine Maitland, shortly after he became lieutenant-governor, added the plum of judge of the Home District Court. Powell retained the three positions until his death in 1838, but neither Maitland nor his successor, Sir John Colborne, singled him out for further favours as they did James FitzGibbon.

Some members of the House of Assembly were annoyed that Maitland had not consulted the Assembly about the change of clerk. The House was not sitting when the two appointments were made, and it was not until January 1828 that the speaker of the Assembly read the official announcement to the House. Immediately afterwards, one of the members, Captain John Matthews, seconded by Thomas Hornor, moved that a committee be appointed to inquire where the right lay of appointing officers of the House. The motion was adopted. The committee included two well-known critics of the government, Dr John Rolph and Marshall Bidwell, as well as the attorney-general, John Beverley Robinson, and one other, a Mr Gordon. Criticism of FitzGibbon's appointment was implicit in the Assembly's action, but the criticism was directed to the lieutenant-governor for his autocratic procedure rather than to James FitzGibbon personally. When the committee reported to the Assembly two months later, it upheld the lieutenant-governor's right to appoint the clerk of the House of Assembly, but it noted disapprovingly that Dr Grant Powell had been removed from his position in the House and appointed clerk of the Legislative Council without any prior consultation with the Assembly. This ended the discussion on the matter.

In his new position as clerk in the House of Assembly, FitzGibbon was entitled to a salary of £180 sterling (£200 currency) a year, the same as he had received as assistant adjutant-general of militia. The House of Assembly increased the amount, however, by adopting the custom of voting an additional sum for "extra services" of the clerk. At first this sum was £90 (sterling), but within a year or two the amount was doubled so that for most of his period as clerk of the Assembly, FitzGibbon received £360 sterling (£400 currency) per annum. The position brought also the less-tangible advantage of greater visibility before important government officials and the public at large. And there was truth in FitzGibbon's own description of the post as "an Appointment of honour in high trust".[1]

In the course of a year, substantial sums of money passed through the clerk's hands for publishing purposes, postage, and other expenses. The 1829 *Journal* of the House of Assembly recorded that warrants amounting to almost £2,000 had been issued by the lieutenant-governor to enable the clerk to pay the contingent expenses of his office for the previous session. Eight years later the sum had quadrupled. Although FitzGibbon was always in debt, he was never accused of misappropriation of funds except on one occasion near the end of his term of office when he went unwisely to England without leave, before paying all the bills due. (This episode will be considered in more detail later). In his regular duties as clerk, FitzGibbon was responsible for recording all motions and proceedings of the House of Assembly and for publishing its *Journal*. He was entitled to appoint and was expected to supervise the work of one or more assistant clerks and copying clerks, those human forerunners of the typewriter and photocopying machine. FitzGibbon performed his duties conscientiously and well, and in his 14 years of office became firmly identified with the House of Assembly.

That did not mean, however, that James had to resign his other posts. He retained his appointments as colonel in the militia and as justice of the peace, Home District, and a year after becoming Assembly clerk, he received still another appointment, that of registrar of the Court of Probate. This court was responsible for the probation of wills and the administration of estates of persons dying intestate in Upper Canada. No salary was attached to the position, but the registrar was entitled to fees, which in FitzGibbon's case ranged from £20 in 1828 to a high of £77 in 1840. The Court of Probate was one of the well-known vehicles of government patronage. Dr Grant Powell, as we have seen, was the official principal of the court while holding two other government positions. FitzGibbon held his office of registrar as long as he was clerk of the Assembly. Both Powell and FitzGibbon were examples of the widespread practice of plurality in Upper Canada, but the most notable example was William Allan, mentioned previously as paymaster of militia claims. This Scottish-born, poorly-educated but extremely successful man served as postmaster at York, collector of customs, inspector of stills and taverns, and treasurer of the Home District, before moving on to become banker, insurance executive, and member of the Legislative and Executive Councils. Allan was an outsider who became an influential member of the Family Compact.

FitzGibbon's appointment to the Court of Probate was probably a reward for a special assignment he carried out for Maitland early in 1828. Like his earlier mission in the Bathurst District, this one concerned dissatisfied immigrants, but in this case, no riot was involved. In some ways the situation called for greater tact than the previous one had. These La Guayra immigrants, as they were called, had gone to Guelph under the sponsorship of the Canada Company, the land company that owned the Huron Tract. The immigrants were destitute on their arrival. Many of them were ill and without money. In order to provide badly-needed services such as food, lodging and medical supplies, the superintendent of the company, John Galt, unofficially "borrowed" £1,000 from money the company owed the Upper Canadian government. (When other company officials learned of this, they rebuked Galt and insisted that he repay the money immediately). Neither the Colonial department in Britain nor the government of Upper Canada had given official approval to the Canada Company for this movement of immigrants. Bad feeling existed between John Galt and Sir Peregrine Maitland, who distrusted Galt and who had to answer to the colonial secretary for what was happening in the province.

Despite the foreign name, the La Guayra settlers were actually a group of Scottish families who had gone to Venezuela (attracted by the rosy promises of a London-based colonization company), only to find after a year or so that they could not make a living. The dry soil and hot climate called for a kind of farming in which they had had no experience – the production of such crops as cotton, sugar and coffee. Negotiations to assist them in their plight were conducted by British officials and others in Venezuela. Finally, the La Guayra settlers (so-called because their settlement was near the harbour of La Guayra on the northern coast of Venezuela) sailed in two ships for the United States. In New York, they were greeted by the British vice-consul, James Clarke Buchanan, who happened also to be the New York agent for the Canada Company. Buchanan arranged for the settlers to proceed to Canada, and in the fall of 1827 they arrived in Guelph, a new town that Galt had founded in April of that year. The group consisted of 23 families, a total of 146 individuals. John Galt did what he could to meet the needs of the poverty-stricken and ailing settlers. He put the men to work building houses for their families and a road to the settlement. This became the Elora Road, and the settlement on lots that bordered the road was known as the Scotch Block.

As winter approached, the settlers became desperate. It was obvious that they would not be able to support themselves for many months, and their debts were mounting. This was a sore point, as the settlers claimed that they had been promised free grants of land from the government as well as other assistance in getting established. They were dismayed when Galt finally explained the terms of settlement: 50 acres of land at 10 shillings per acre for each head of a family, with an option to buy an adjoining 50 acres. Moreover, they were expected to pay the cost of building their houses and buying their equipment. Four of the settlers brought matters to a head by sending a petition to the lieutenant-governor, stating their complaints and asking for free grants of land. The Executive Council set up an inquiry into the affair. As part of the inquiry, Maitland asked James FitzGibbon and John Radenhurst, a clerk in the surveyor-general's office, to make a first-hand investigation in Guelph. They did this early in January 1828.

FitzGibbon and Radenhurst interviewed about 20 heads of families in the presence of Canada Company officials, as they tried to sort out the complicated story of why and how the immigrants had come to Upper Canada, what terms the Canada Company expected them to meet, and what assistance the settlers wanted from the provincial government. The investigators persuaded the four settlers who had written the offending petition to withdraw it. All the settlers then agreed to sign and present another petition which James FitzGibbon wrote for them, in more diplomatic language, describing how their unfortunate situation had developed, and why they had expected to receive free grants of land. In their report to Maitland, FitzGibbon and Radenhurst reviewed the immigrants' movements from Scotland to Venezuela and then to Upper Canada, explained how the misunderstanding about the terms of settlement had arisen, and expressed confidence that the settlers would accept a reasonable solution to their problems and would conduct themselves peaceably.

When the Executive Council made its report of the

inquiry, Maitland was exonerated from the charge of inaction. It was decided that the provincial government had no further responsibility for the immigrants, since the Canada Company was looking after them, and that no free grants of land should be given to them.

The outcome of the inquiry was very disappointing to the La Guayra settlers, who continued to suffer hardships for two years or more. But in time, their farming efforts proved successful, and the Scotch Block settlers are now honoured as the pioneers of Guelph township. As for James FitzGibbon, he had once again performed well as an investigator and mediator, had soothed the feelings of the unhappy settlers, and had helped to extricate Maitland from an embarrassing situation.

Maitland showed his approval of FitzGibbon's conduct in September 1828, by appointing him registrar of the Court of Probate. Sir Peregine soon left Upper Canada to become lieutenant-governor of Nova Scotia. For the second time in his life, James FitzGibbon suffered the loss of a beneficent patron. Once again, as when General Brock moved on to a higher post, he had cause to wonder what the future might hold in store for him. It would depend, of course, on the attitude of the new lieutenant-governor. He was Sir John Colborne, a major-general like Maitland, and like him, a distinguished veteran of the Battle of Waterloo. Indeed, Colborne was credited with having led an action that made the victory at Waterloo possible. Previously, he had served with the British army at the Helder in Holland in the 1799 compaign in which young Sergeant FitzGibbon, just two years younger than Colborne, had been taken prisoner. Colborne had the distinction of having won his promotions by merit, without purchase, and he had a disabled arm that testified to his service.

FitzGibbon was not alone in wondering what his fate might be under the new governor. The *Canadian Freeman* commented sarcastically: "Now every one knows that FitzGibbon was a pet of Sir Peregrine's, a leading hack that could do almost anything with impunity in those days of pimping sycophancy . . . . But Sir John Colborne has a character at stake and we hope he will not allow

Sir John Colborne, 1st Baron Seaton, Lieutenant-Governor of Upper Canada, 1828-1836

himself to be hoodwinked in this way" . . . .[2] "Hoodwinked" or not, Lieutenant-Governor Colborne not only prolonged or renewed the appointments FitzGibbon already held, but he added other responsibilities as well. He came to rely on FitzGibbon for special services even more than Maitland had done. As for the implication that FitzGibbon was a sycophant, the judgment was too harsh. FitzGibbon was perhaps overly respectful to his superiors, as was customary in his day. But he was never servile, and he was capable of expressing strong disagreement, even with Colborne, as well as his successor Sir Francis Bond Head. As a military man, FitzGibbon had a genuine admiration for Sir John Colborne. It is also true, however, that he had become well-practised in the art of pleasing a lieutenant-govenor. In this, he succeeded well with Colborne, within limits.

Apart from his brilliant record as an army officer, Colborne had acquired the reputation of being a good administrator in his previous position as lieutenant-governor of Guernsey. In Upper Canada, he was more inclined than Maitland to follow his own judgment in resolving problems, and he placed less reliance on the advice of the Family Compact. He pleased the people of the province by his unpretentious manner and style of living, which lacked the ostentation associated with Sir Peregrine Maitland.

Colborne had been in Upper Canada less than two months when he expressed disagreement with Archdeacon John Strachan over the latter's plan to establish a university, King's College, at York. This was to be an Anglican university endowed by the provincial government. The lieutenant-governor was to be its chancellor, and the archdeacon of York (that is, Strachan) its president. Maitland had assisted in obtaining a royal charter. But Colborne considered it ridiculous to provide a university before there was a good grammar school to prepare prospective students for it. He told Strachan that he could not sanction the founding of King's College until the Royal Grammar School of York was converted into an excellent secondary school. Upper Canada College was the result. This school for boys, which incorporated the Royal Grammar School (formerly the Home District

Grammar School), was modelled on the English public schools and in particular on Elizabeth College in Guernsey, a boys' school that Colborne had reorganized while in that colony. Upper Canada College opened in January 1830 with an enrolment of 89 boys, among whom were four FitzGibbons – Charles, George, William and James. It was a proud day for their father, who was determined that his sons would have a better education than he.

Upper Canada College has proved its worth as a fruitful training ground for leaders in professional and government circles, but in 1830 some citizens of York questioned the suitability of its classical curriculum for boys in a community where tradesmen and mechanics were needed as much as professionals. The school appealed particularly to the privileged few who could afford to have their sons go to university or train for a profession. James FitzGibbon was hardly in that category; nevertheless he was willing to pay the fee of £8 per year for each son enrolled at the college. (All his sons, except George who died young, eventually studied law). No doubt FitzGibbon was also conscious of the social advantages attached to Upper Canada College. There was a note of snobbishness in the pleasure he expressed some years later when he told of meeting Colborne in Montreal (after he had ceased to be lieutenant-governor), and how Colborne "condescended to inquire after my children individually for he knew them individually, His Excellency's sons having attended Upper Canada College at the same time as my sons did".[3]

Evidently Colborne was pleased with FitzGibbon's support of Upper Canada College, for he put him on the building committee for the new quarters on Russell Square, where the college moved in 1831. Later, Colborne appointed FitzGibbon a trustee of the Home District Public School.

It will be recalled that at the time of the trouble in the Bathurst District, FitzGibbon blamed the Orangemen for the violence that had occurred. Perhaps he exaggerated the role of the Orangemen, but if so, it was because he feared that the conflict between Catholics and militant Protestants that had plagued Ireland for so long was being transferred to Canada. In Perth, the Orange society continued to grow under the leadership of the deputy sheriff, Alexander Matheson, and this situation, combined with the danger of a confrontation between Orange Protestants and Irish Catholics in the Newcastle District, led FitzGibbon to address an open letter "To the Orangemen of Cavan and Perth". FitzGibbon printed and distributed this 3-page pamphlet at his own expense, in the summer of 1826. It was an appeal to the Orange lodges of the two settlements not to march in procession on 12 July as they intended. FitzGibbon declared that whereas in the past, it might have been necessary for Protestants to organize into societies for self-defence. he could not now see "one justifiable reason for your continuing to go abroad in processions, which have ever been considered by your Catholic fellow Subjects as offensive and insulting to them in the highest degree". He entreated his fellow Irishmen "to cultivate peace and good will towards each other".[4] The letter did not bring an end to Orange processions, and it was only a matter of time before FitzGibbon became involved again in the Orange-Catholic conflict.

Before that happened, however, FitzGibbon's sentiments on the Orange question led to his involvement in a customs scandal. This came about when he tried to help a fellow Irishman, William Bergin, who shared his dislike of the Orange societies. Bergin, a prominent Roman Catholic merchant in York and one-time agent for Mackenzie's *Colonial Advocate*, had sponsored a petition opposing Orange lodges as early as 1822, when the Orangemen paraded in York. His petition led to the introduction of a bill in the House of Assembly "against Orange societies and other party distinctions", which was debated in the Assembly but not passed. Bergin followed this up with another petition that led to a second anti-Orange bill in 1824, but it too was defeated. Some years later, Bergin became implicated in a customs dispute that had nothing to do with the Orange society, but his sympathetic friend James FitzGibbon undertook to help him out nevertheless. The trouble arose over a shipment of pork seized by the customs officer at Port Hope, Marcus Whitehead. Whitehead claimed that Bergin had smuggled it across the border from the United States. The merchant denied the charge and asked FitzGibbon to intercede for him. Bergin convinced the latter that he was not guilty of smuggling the pork, whereupon FitzGibbon entered into negotiations with Whitehead. They reached an agreement whereby Bergin would pay Whitehead £75 to cover the expenses incurred by the customs officer when he allegedly went to Rochester to obtain evidence. In return, the customs officer agreed to give back the pork. The money was delivered to Whitehead by FitzGibbon's brother-in-law, Simon Washburn, a well-known York lawyer who acted as Bergin's legal representative.

When the transaction became known it caused a scandal. Whitehead was dismissed from his post and the York newspapers filled their columns with the story. It appeared from the newspapers, however, that there was more than one reason for Whitehead's dismissal. A petition, signed by several inhabitants of the Newcastle District, had called for his resignation on various grounds such as wrongly seizing a vessel belonging to a local lake captain, being too lenient with a friend accused of smuggling tea, and finally, for having accepted the sum of £75 in lieu of the pork seized from William Bergin. It was the Bergin case that drew sparks from Francis Collins, editor of the *Canadian Freeman*, who declared in an editorial, "If Mr. Whitehead has been bribed at all, it was done by two government officers in this town, and if it be necessary to dismiss a public officer, for taking a bribe, it is, *a fortiore*, necessary to dismiss the government officers who gave it, for we think the latter by far the more culpable".[5]

The government officers that Collins had in mind were, of course, Assembly Clerk James FitzGibbon and the lawyer, Simon Washburn, who was clerk of the peace, Home District.

The controversy was stirred up further by an affidavit that Marcus Whitehead prepared in defence of his action, accompanied by a "certificate" of explanation written, at his request, by James FitzGibbon. The two statements were published in the local papers. FitzGibbon said in his certificate:

> I will here state that for two years previously I had exerted myself to persuade the Orangemen to decline appearing in public procession, and in the course of my proceedings to accomplish this object, I learned that the Roman Catholics had one year made arrangements to offer resistance to the Orangemen. I therefore, addressed myself to some of the most influential men among them, and succeeded in dissuading them from their purpose. Mr Bergin was most zealous and successful in aiding me in my efforts to pacify the Roman Catholics, until at length to the credit of both parties, peace was established between them. When Mr Bergin applied to me to intercede with Mr Whitehead, and assured me that he had not smuggled the Pork in question, I made every inquiry in my power until I was satisfied of the fact.

This statement greatly offended the Roman Catholics. They resented particularly the implication that they had threatened to disturb the peace. They called a public meeting to refute the charge made by FitzGibbon, whom they called "an apostate". At the meeting, they passed a resolution declaring that FitzGibbon's certificate was "a gross libel on the Roman Catholic population of the place", and they prepared an address to Colborne, assuring His Excellency that the Roman Catholics of York "never contemplated anything but a peaceable demeanor towards 'the Orangemen' ". Colborne, on accepting the address, replied, "Gentlemen, I shall always feel happy to receive any communication correcting *erroneous* statements".[6] This equivocal response pleased the Catholics without actually condemning FitzGibbon who, indeed, had written previously to Colborne's secretary Zacariah Mudge, explaining his part in the Whitehead affair. He told Mudge that he had been induced to act on behalf of Bergin because of "the aid he very properly and readily afforded me in abating the hostile feelings which recently existed between the Orange Men and the Roman Catholics in this District", adding that Bergin had worked also on behalf of needy Irish immigrants as secretary of the "Strangers' Friend Society" (Society for the Relief of Strangers in Distress). "Beyond these I had no imaginable motive to favor Mr Bergin".[7] Whatever Colborne may have thought privately of the Assembly clerk's indiscreet interference in the customs seizure, he gave no sign of any loss of confidence in him.

When a dangerous riot occurred in York about two years after the customs scandal, Colborne had good reason to be grateful to FitzGibbon for the speedy action he took to quell the violence. He did this in his role as justice of the peace or magistrate. Although he had been a justice of the peace since 1820, FitzGibbon had not always been active as such, and in July 1830 he offered to resign as magistrate after a citizen of York lodged a complaint against him for inadequate protection to some property. He explained in his letter to Colborne's secretary that he had not known in advance that Maitland intended to appoint him a justice of the peace, and he said that he had regretted it at the time because he was always fully occupied with his official duties and domestic affairs and had felt that he could "ill afford to make the latter give way to new and unremunerated Services". (Justices of the peace received no salary). He had felt also, FitzGibbon said, that he did not have the necessary knowledge or experience to perform efficiently as a magistrate. His sense of duty had prevailed, however, and he had decided upon reflection that he could learn to qualify by his own efforts. But when the pressure of his work in the militia office had become so great as to require all his time, he had asked Lieutenant-Governor Maitland to relieve him of his magisterial appointment. Instead of allowing FitzGibbon to resign, Maitland had authorized him to withdraw from the ordinary duties of the magistracy while continuing to hold the position, so that he could be "employed as such on any extraordinary or peculiar occasion", when his services might be required. This was a reference, presumably, to the possibility of an outbreak of violence such as the riot that had occurred in the Bathurst District. FitzGibbon had therefore remained an inactive magistrate until after his appointment as clerk of the Assembly when he found, he said, that he was under less pressure than in his former post and, "seeing that the duty fell heavily on the few Magistrates who act in this Town, I again obeyed the usual calls". FitzGibbon told Mudge that he was willing to resign but preferred not to.

"I know that I have been said to aspire to situations and offices without regard to my want of the necesssary Education and intelligence to qualify me for properly discharging the duties appertaining to them", he said, adding that his chief ambition had "ever been to discharge my public duties with the utmost fidelity and zeal".[8] Colborne did not accept his offer of resignation.

There was a striking coincidence about the timing of FitzGibbon's decision to resume his activity as justice of the peace in 1827 and the passing of a law that same year by the Upper Canada Legislature setting forth the fees permissible to magistrates. According to this legislation, the magistrates could henceforth collect fees for such duties as issuing warrants and subpoenas, and making convictions. Although some fees had been allowed in the past, the magistrates had not been adequately remunerated. The new law undoubtedly made the magistracy more attractive to FitzGibbon, who was always in need of money.

The political riot that erupted in York in March 1832 showed FitzGibbon at the peak of his effectiveness as a magistrate. The Scottish rebel William Lyon Mackenzie was at the centre of the trouble. By this time, Mackenzie was in politics. In 1828 he was elected as one of two members of the Assembly from York county. In the House, Mackenzie was disruptive with his continual barrage of complaints. He criticized the Post Office, the Bank of Upper Canada, the Welland Canal Company and other projects dear to the government party, thus setting the stage for the series of his Assembly expulsions and re-elections that made a mockery of the democratic process from 1831 to 1834. After the House of Assembly prorogued in late January 1832, Mackenzie went out to the rural areas, mingled with the people, listened to their grievances, and agitated for reform. The Tory leaders reacted by setting up committees to counteract the influence of the radicals. In Hamilton, a violent attack was made on Mackenzie. Following a public meeting that he had addressed in that city, two men, George Pettit and William J. Kerr, called upon Mackenzie at the house where he was staying. They persuaded him to step outside for a word in private and there, at the front door, three ruffians assaulted him, knocked him down, kicked and beat him until he was rescued by his friends.

Mackenzie still had a black eye and a bandaged nose when he attended a political meeting in York a few days later. This meeting had been advertised by the Reformers as an opportunity for the inhabitants of York to express to His Majesty's Government their sentiments on the state of the colony and its government. The Tories took the notice as a challenge to them, and they urged loyal citizens to attend the meeting and help put down "the demagogues". When the crowd assembled in front of the courthouse on King Street on March 23, the Tories outnumbered the Reformers and they easily took control of the meeting. The Reformers, not to be outdone by the Tories, moved across the square to the jail to hold their own meeting. Using for platform a farm wagon in which were placed a table and two chairs, the chairman, Jesse Ketchum, opened the meeting and called on Mackenzie to speak. Mackenzie had hardly begun when he had to dodge a shower of stones and other missiles that were hurled at him. Some of the ringleaders, said to be Irish youths, seized the wagon and started pulling it along the street. The sheriff, William Botsford Jarvis, succeeded in restoring peace temporarily by persuading the Tories to parade in a triumphal march to Government House, a few blocks to the west on King Street.

While the Tories paraded, the Reformers resumed their meeting, condemned the resolutions that had been adopted by the Tories and passed some of their own. When they heard the paraders returning, they hastened to adjourn. Meanwhile, another group of Tories had prepared an effigy of Mackenzie which they carried about the streets. The two Tory groups joined forces and proceeded to the office of the *Colonial Advocate* on Church Street. There they burned the effigy in the street.

The scene turned violent. Fighting began, windows were broken, and a shot was fired from the *Advocate* building by one of Mackenzie's apprentices. Fortunately, the shot hurt no one (some said the gun was loaded with type), but the violence increased. The rioters tried to force their way into the *Advocate* office. At this point, Magistrate FitzGibbon stepped in and took command of the

King Street East, Toronto, 1835. Left to right: Jail, Court House, St. James Anglican Church

situation. None of the other magistrates came to his assistance. Newspapers reports varied on how he quelled the riot, but here is his own account:

> . . . a shot was fired from one of the windows [of the *Advocate* office] and a rush was made into the office. I instantly pressed thro' the Crowd calling aloud for every good man to aid me in keeping the peace. I seized the principal Rioter and dragged him rapidly to the jail, which was near at hand, returned and took another, and for more than one hour I had to struggle with the greatest difficulty, but in the end suppressed the tumult completely. In the midst of the turmoil Mr Mackenzie demanded of me to call out the Troops. To which I answered "No, Sir, I shall find good men enough to aid me in keeping the Peace, but I recommend you to retire to your house, for you are the chief cause of the riot". He answered "I will not, Sir, I have as good a right to be here as you". I then said "I will put you in jail if you do not". He answered "You dare not, I am a Member of Parliament", whereupon I seized him and pulled him towards the jail until the crowd so surrounded me that I could not advance further. Seeing near two friends of him, also Members of the Assembly, I appealed to them saying that I had no wish to imprison him if he would retire to his house, and requested of them to take him home and that I would protect them while doing so, and they complied. But before moving I turned to the crowd and said aloud, "Mr. Mackenzie calls upon me to order out the Troops! but I will not insult you by complying with his demand. I will call upon you, and you, and you" turning round the while, and pointing to individuals "and find good men enough to ensure the King's Peace". I was answered with a shout of approbation, and I then conducted Mr Mackenzie to his house and shut him in, having at the door to use force, he endeavouring to address the multitude which I would not permit.[9]

Thus the tall, muscular magistrate disposed of the little fiery politician and brought the crisis to an end.

There remained a threatening air of excitement in town, and some citizens feared that fighting would erupt again through the night. The Reformers appealed to the lieutenant-governor to send troops into town to help keep the peace. FitzGibbon advised otherwise: "I pray of Your Excellency not to send a man". He argued shrewdly that "It is a great object with Mr Mackenzie and his Party to have the Troops called out, for they have been outnumbered and beaten this day, and they now desire to have the Troops called out that they may proclaim tomorrow to the Province that but for the interference of the Troops they would have triumphed".[10] Colborne accepted his advice. FitzGibbon and some special constables remained at the court house all night, but no further outbreak occurred. Mackenzie left for England the following month and remained there a year trying to pressure the British government to introduce reforms in Upper Canada and to recall Lieutenant-Governor Colborne.

In the summer of 1832, during a serious outbreak of cholera, James FitzGibbon performed selflessly for the lieutenant-governor and the province. The disease erupted first in Québec and Montréal, where it was brought by shiploads of immigrants. Soon it spread to Upper Canada. Colborne acted quickly and efficiently to take charge of the dangerous situation. He directed the magistrates of each district in the province to set up boards of health to enforce sanitary regulations and establish hospitals. In the Home District, the magistrates established the York Board of Health consisting of all the doctors of the town and several laymen. The York General Hospital was converted into a cholera hospital. Throughout the summer, ships continued to arrive with immigrants, presenting a constant and frightening threat of further outbreaks of the disease. "About 11,000 Emigrants have arrived at York, Cobourg, and the head of the Lake this season", Colborne wrote to the colonial secretary, Lord Goderich, in July, "and I have found it necessary to make every exertion to prevent an accumulation of them at this Port".[11] To do this, he placed James FitzGibbon in charge of immigrant dispersal at York. As emigrants arrived, they were met at the harbour and transported to other centres in the province where they were able to obtain work on road construction (initiated by Colborne for this purpose), until such time as they could proceed to the new townships or other destinations. For this onerous, disagreeable and dangerous task, FitzGibbon was allowed ten shillings per day for expenses, a sum that proved far from adequate. In the course of his work that summer, FitzGibbon gave over £100 of his own money to help cholera victims.

Years later, FitzGibbon described his efforts in a memorial to Sir Francis Bond Head, writing in the third person as was the custom:

> He purchased a Horse for this service and rode from his House every morning at Eight o'Clock, returning twice or thrice rapidly during each day to change his dress, required by the extreme heat of the weather, and to take some light refreshment, but continuing employed until eleven and twelve o'Clock at night; it being part of his arrangement to have the dead buried after sunset. And as in many cases no Clergyman could be found disengaged from their own several Church burying grounds Memorialist read the Service over those interred in the new burying ground prepared for that great emergency. The exertions made on this occasion proved too much for him, and illness confined him to his House for a few weeks at the close of the Season.[12]

The worst of the cholera epidemic was over by the fall of 1832. It had taken a toll of over 200 lives in York. The York Board of Health was disbanded. The following April, Sir John Colborne appointed a new board for York and vicinity, with James FitzGibbon as one of its eight members. And so, to FitzGibbon's other responsibilities, public health was added.

FitzGibbon now held five public offices, in addition to that of colonel in the militia. These were: clerk of the Assembly, justice of the peace, registrar of the Court of Probate, member of the York Board of Health, and commissioner (one of three) to superintend the completion of the new Parliament Building. The last was an appointment made earlier in the year by the House of Assembly. A more surprising appointment, in view of FitzGibbon's previous involvement in the customs scandal, came in July 1833 when Colborne named James FitzGibbon as one of three commissioners of customs for the Home District (the others were Robert Stanton and William Hepburn). Their duty was to examine information and complaints about customs seizures worth up to £40. They were to hold office during "pleasure", and they were entitled to certain fees, rights and privileges.

Colborne may have given the customs commission post to FitzGibbon as compensation for being rejected for another position that he had applied for earlier that year, the position of inspector-general of public provincial accounts. This position became vacant on the death of James Baby, who had been inspector-general since 1815. FitzGibbon's application for the post was a perfect example of his alleged aspiration for offices for which he lacked the proper qualifications, a charge that he himself had commented on in his letter to Zachariah Mudge. How could a man who had always failed so woefully to match his personal expenditures to his income hope to assume the responsibility for provincial funds? In his role as clerk of the Assembly he was, of course, responsible for handling public money, but it was done within the strict limitations of a budget voted by the Assembly. Even if Colborne had wished to consider FitzGibbon for the post of inspector-general, he would surely have hesitated to do so in view of a memorial that he had received from FitzGibbon a year earlier.

The purpose of that memorial was to request a grant of land in recognition of his service as captain of the Incorporated Militia Battalion in 1814. (The request was refused, as FitzGibbon had already received 800 acres as an army captain and an additional 400 acres as a militia colonel). FitzGibbon supported his request for land by outlining his services in the army and for the government, and, strangely, by describing the course of his debts. The sale of his captain's commission in 1825 had enabled him to discharge his debts "then exceeding £1600", he said, but he had again become financially embarrassed and "at this time, he [the memorialist] is pressed down by debt almost beyond endurance".[13] It was not a statement that would inspire confidence in the memorialist's ability to perform well as inspector-general of provincial accounts. Colborne chose George Herchmer Markland for the post. Markland had worked with Colborne in the creation of Upper Canada College. He was the son of a United Empire Loyalist, a member of both the Executive and Legislative Councils, and, like many members of the governing circle, he had attended John Strachan's school for boys in Cornwall. Markland had the advantages that FitzGibbon lacked: loyalist ancestry, a prosperous family background (his father was a Kingston merchant), an acceptable education, and friends with prestige and influence, such as Archdeacon Strachan and John Beverley Robinson.

Although James FitzGibbon was handicapped in his ambition by his lack of such advantages, he was distinguished by qualities that came to the fore in dangerous situations like the political riot in York. Those qualities included his military bearing, his height, physical strength, his courage and his popularity with ordinary people. When the latent hostility between the Orangemen and the Catholics turned to violence on 12 July 1833, FitzGibbon rose to the occasion again, and was largely responsible for restoring order. Seven years had passed since he had addressed his open letter to the Orangemen of Cavan and Perth, and while Orange parades had taken place in those and other centres, there had been none in York, due partly at least, to the influence of FitzGibbon.

By July 1833 the situation had changed. As FitzGibbon explained it, in his memorial to Sir Francis Head, previously mentioned, "some newly arrived Orangemen persuaded a few of the less discreet of those already in the Province to join them in procession on the 12th of July, and they marched thro' the City into the country on the morning of that day; and although Memorialist rode after them into the Country and took every possible precaution in his power to prevent collision, yet on their return they were encountered by the catholics when the Riot . . . took place." FitzGibbon thought that this riot was potentially more dangerous than the earlier political riot had been. The *Colonial Advocate* described the violence as follows:

> . . . the Catholics became quite infuriated and . . . commenced a hostile attack, some with *walloping-poles* in hand, some with hammers, some with other weapons and some without any, which compliment was returned by the orangemen in Irish style. The magistrates promptly interfered and after dragging some twenty or thirty of the combattants to jail, succeeded in quelling the riot.[14]

Foremost among the magistrates was Colonel James FitzGibbon who, judging from the newspaper accounts, stopped the rioting by strong-arm methods. George Gurnett, editor of the *Courier of Upper Canada*, thought that FitzGibbon's efforts were excessive, but neither the *Colonial Advocate* nor *The Patriot* agreed. "With respect to Mr. Gurnett's censures on Col. FitzGibbon", *The Patriot* said, "we can only observe that they are at variance with the generally expressed opinion, his conduct being the theme of universal praise"; and the *Colonial Advocate* defended FitzGibbon and the other magistrates, saying, "we are . . . inclined to attribute any overt act of theirs [the magistrates] rather to a want of the time requisite for reflection than to any ill design".[15]

It was an odd turn of events for the *Colonial Advocate* to defend the magistrates and James FitzGibbon in particular, but the newspaper's benevolent attitude could perhaps be explained by the continued absence of its editor in England. (Mackenzie returned later in the summer). Two years prior to the riot, the *Colonial Advocate* had waged a campaign against the magistracy: the way the justices of the peace were chosen, their excessive powers and their lack of accountability to the public. Mackenzie had fired some of his sharpest barbs at "Judge FitzGibbon", particularly for his part as investigator in the case of York shopkeeper Robert Cosway, who had been charged with selling rum illegally after being denied a liquor licence. While in England, Mackenzie sent copies of this series of articles, and the newspaper correspondence that followed, to Lord Goderich, the colonial secretary, as part of his campaign to persuade the British government to recall Sir John Colborne. Mackenzie claimed that many magistrates were incompetent but nevertheless controlled local affairs, disposed of the taxes paid by the farmers and others, and sat in judgment over offences against the law. In order to be appointed a justice of the peace, he said, a man must share the political opinions of the government.

Mackenzie's complaints about the magistracy were largely justified. The justices of the peace in a district met quarterly in a Court of Quarter Sessions to deal with minor infractions of the law, to regulate the district finances, to supervise the jails and courthouses, and to attend to other municipal matters. The lieutenant-governor appointed the magistrates, usually on the advice of prominent citizens of the district, but he had difficulty in finding suitable candidates who were willing to act. It was not uncommon for magistrates to remain inactive, as FitzGibbon had done on the suggestion of Lieutenant-Governor Maitland. Many men who were appointed failed to take the oath of office or to perform their duties. The fees were not sufficiently large to attract and hold some of the most highly qualified candidates.

James FitzGibbon was a magistrate of the Home District for about 20 years, and in that period he served three times as chairman of the Court of Quarter Sessions. He symbolized for Mackenzie some of the worst features of Colborne's administration. "He [Colborne] has placed or retained individuals in a plurality of offices, the several duties of which were evidently incompatible with each other", Mackenzie stated, pointing to FitzGibbon as an example: "Clerk of the House of Assembly, Chairman of the Quarter Sessions, register of the Court of Probate, Superintendant of College Buildings, Justice of the Peace &c". When FitzGibbon wrote a letter to the *Colonial Advocate* defending his actions in the Cosway case and denying Mackenzie's charges that fines were levied unfairly and that the lieutenant-governor benefitted from the fines, Mackenzie retorted with an acid comment suggesting that His Excellency had solicited FitzGibbon's services to explain away the "remarks which to him might appear personal", and he launched into stinging criticism of the magistracy: "To enable a snug little nest of clerks and other public servants for hire, residing at York, under the pretended and deceptious style and title of 'the Magistracy of the Home District' to engross power, to drag before them his majesty's subjects . . .", and so on. Finally, coming to James FitzGibbon, Mackenzie said,

> As to FitzGibbon we must say that we think him a very useful functionary in the capacity of Assembly's Clerk; as the principal servant of the Commons' House he is attentive to his duty and civil and obliging in his department. We have every reason to be satisfied with

> him. But he should confine himself to his desk, for it is really too much for human patience to see a few personal dependents on a governor — clerks in offices, auditors of the revenue & persons who work for hire — enabled to usurp the station of an independent magistracy for a district containing upwards of thirty thousand souls, and thus to insult the sense of the freeholders, squander their revenues, trample under foot their petitions. . . . If Mr FitzGibbon is really the chosen friend and confident [*sic*] of the Lieutenant Governor, he had better advise him to revise his system, seek a more independent chairman [of the Quarter Sessions], and now and then condescend to follow the example of his sovereign by endeavouring to ascertain the sense of the people.[16]

Although Colborne had already taken some steps to improve the magistracy, they had been inadequate. He ignored Mackenzie's advice and he left FitzGibbon with all his positions intact.

William Lyon Mackenzie returned to Upper Canada disillusioned about appeals to the Mother Country. Although the colonial secretary, Lord Goderich, had encouraged him to present his complaints, and Mackenzie had responded with voluminous documentation, in the end he realized that his mission had accomplished little. His efforts to have Colborne recalled came to nothing. The Family Compact remained firmly in power and the government's administrative practices continued as before.

The farce of Mackenzie's re-elections and expulsions was repeated after his return to Upper Canada. When he attempted to take his seat in the House of Assembly in November 1833 as the re-elected member for the second riding of York, James FitzGibbon as clerk of the Assembly refused to administer the Oath of Allegiance, as did the clerk of the Crown in Chancery, Samuel Peters Jarvis. FitzGibbon gave as his reason that "because [Mackenzie] had been expelled again from the House, subsequently to that re-election, I could not consider him as a Member". In so acting, FitzGibbon took a stand with the Tory faction of the House, though he was, supposedly, the impartial servant of all members. Lieutenant-Governor

Colborne tried to resolve the impasse by instructing the clerk of the Executive Council to administer the oath. This was done, and Mackenzie appeared in the House of Assembly on 11 February 1834 only to be seized by the sergeant-at-arms, admonished by the speaker, Archibald McLean, and discharged from the House. In sharp contrast with this rude treatment was the honour bestowed upon Mackenzie by the citizens of the newly-incorporated city of Toronto (formerly York), who elected him an alderman and, by subsequent vote of the aldermen, first mayor of Toronto. In the provincial election of October 1834, Mackenzie was once again elected to represent the York second riding, and this time was permitted to take his seat.

Mackenzie was far from cowed by these repeated expulsions from the Assembly. He quickly resumed his role as radical reformer, and soon was appointed chairman of the Select Committee on Grievances. This gave him the pleasure of summoning government officials and other witnesses to answer his probing questions. The final or *Seventh Report* on his findings was a shattering attack on the Family Compact and an exposure of government patronage. It alarmed Lord Glenelg, the new colonial secretary in Britain, who decided to recall Sir John Colborne. He did not do so immediately, however, but the tone of his despatches to Colborne left the latter in no doubt about the colonial secretary's displeasure. Colborne resigned early in December 1835. About the same time, Glenelg wrote to inform him that he would be replaced. The two letters crossed in mid-ocean. Colborne suffered the embarrassment of hearing that Sir Francis Bond Head had landed in New York before he had received official notice of the appointment. Colborne considered Lord Glenelg unfair, since Mackenzie's report on grievances had not yet been adopted by the Upper Canada House of Assembly (this happened on 6 February 1836). In Colborne's view, the report should not, in any case, have been taken so seriously, as he considered it full of falsehoods and compiled by a demagogue.

A face-saving factor for Colborne was that he had assumed the command of the armed forces of Upper and Lower Canada the previous September when the former commander, Governor-in-Chief Lord Aylmer, had returned to England. Colborne had done this because of the political crisis that he could see was shaping up in the two Canadas, a situation that made it dangerous for the provinces to have no military commander. When Head arrived in Toronto, Major-General Colborne simply moved to Montreal as commander of the forces. He intended to remain there only until a new military commander would be appointed, or until the spring navigation season opened. Consequently, around the middle of May 1836, Colborne left Montreal for New York on his way to England. In New York, however, he received a message from Lord Glenelg appointing him commander of the forces in Upper and Lower Canada, with the rank of lieutenant-general. After a tour of the United States, Colborne returned to Montreal to resume his command, now made official by the British government. He was thus in a strong position when the rebellions of 1837 erupted in Upper and Lower Canada.

Mackenzie's efforts to unseat Colborne as lieutenant-governor had succeeded at last, but the next scenario was not quite as he had envisioned. Sir Francis Bond Head failed to bring reform, and within two years the drama of rebellion unfolded.

Chapter Six

Preferment Denied

With the departure of Sir John Colborne, FitzGibbon lost his last benefactor in Upper Canada. Neither Sir Francis Bond Head nor his successor, Sir George Arthur, had any rapport with James FitzGibbon, and in the case of Head, the two men actually clashed during the Rebellion of 1837. FitzGibbon, however, persisted in applying for high government posts whenever opportunity offered. The perceptive historian J.C. Dent, said that James FitzGibbon "was a persistent seeker after office, because he was almost always in pecuniary straits".[1] His debts weighed heavily on his mind, but FitzGibbon seemed incapable of discharging them or controlling his expenditures.

There were two basic causes of FitzGibbon's increasing indebtedness: his generosity and his pride. He did not have the pride of disdain but the pride of self-esteem, the pride in doing things the right way. His generosity came to the fore during the cholera epidemic when he risked his life on behalf of the victims, bought a horse to enable him to carry out his duties more efficiently, and donated £100 of his own money to assist the afflicted. His sense of pride in appropriate action led him to buy a horse in his partisan days during the War of 1812, though the regulations did not allow for one. Pride in his family led him to the expense of sending his sons to Upper Canada College. Both generosity and pride in his good name led to a costly libel suit that he lost in 1829. The case involved a discharged employee of the Canada Company. This man, whose name was Grant, sued the company for damages, claiming that his dismissal had been stated in terms that defamed his character. The case was referred to arbitration, but suitable arbitrators were hard to find. Finally, James FitzGibbon and Robert Stanton (King's Printer and editor of the *Upper Canada Gazette*) were persuaded to act, out of a sense of duty. They judged in favour of the company, but they also awarded a small sum to Grant on the grounds that while his dismissal had been justified, disparaging language had been used against him. Knowing that their decision would be controversial, the two arbitrators set down their reasons in writing. They gave a copy of their statement to Grant for his information, asking him to return it after perusal. Instead, Grant took the statement to the *York Observer*, whereupon the paper made a violent attack on the two men. FitzGibbon and Stanton then launched action for libel against the proprietor of the newspaper. They lost the case and each had to pay costs of nearly £70.

Despite his sense of family pride, FitzGibbon could not be accused of striving for personal grandeur. He and his family lived in an unpretentious house in Toronto on the corner of Lot and Brock (Queen and Spadina) Streets, which Scadding described as "a modest dwelling-place of wood – somewhat peculiar in expression; square, and rather tall for its depth and width; of dingy hue; its roof four-sided; below, a number of lean-to's and irregular extensions clustering round; in front low shrubbery, a circular drive, and a wide, open-barred gate".[2] Fitzgibbon's granddaughter, Mary Agnes FitzGibbon, gave a picture of happy family life, in which the father was one of the boys with his sons. She described the enjoyment with which he spurred the boys on in a race to be first to enter the new Upper Canada College on Russell Square, the day it opened. As they walked along the lakeshore towards the college, they caught sight of some other boys approaching from the opposite direction. "Run, boys, and we'll beat them", FitzGibbon said, running along beside them. The FitzGibbons won, but by "little more than a neck", as one of the boys put it. "And my father was prouder of that half-dozen steps than if we had beaten by a dozen yards", he said.[3] There was also a strong bond of affection and devotion between father and daughter Mary, as would be shown years later in FitzGibbon's old age. Regrettably, the mother of this happy family was frail, worn out from having given birth to seventeen children, only five of whom survived childhood. Her health deteriorated further after the death of her son George, aged only sixteen. That was a shock from which Mary Haley FitzGibbon never fully recovered.

George's death was caused by a horrifying accident that occurred in 1834 at a political meeting in the St Lawrence market building in Toronto, when one end of the gallery gave way, impaling some unfortunate victims on the butchers' hooks below. George was one of the victims. The red-brick market building, which had been opened the previous year, had an auditorium with a wooden gallery above the butchers' stalls. The crash of the gallery may have been caused by the stamping of feet in applause. Several people suffered broken bones, others had severe lacerations or internal injuries. James FitzGibbon was badly bruised and had his clothes torn off his back. But his concern over his own condition was lost in the anguish of watching his son suffer agonizingly for some hours before death came as a release.

James FitzGibbon was then in his early fifties. He still retained an erect military bearing but had lost some of his resilience. He had difficulty maintaining his good nature and optimism in the face of repeated frustration as he strove for advancement. Before Sir John Colborne left Upper Canada in January 1836, FitzGibbon wrote to him, expressing his disappointment that the lieutenant-governor had not promoted him to a better position, and requesting favourable mention to Colborne's successor. A polite but disappointing reply came from Colborne's secretary, William Rowan.

> With reference to your Communication of the 12th Instant, I am directed by the Lt. Governor to assure you that His Excellency is so fully persuaded of your zeal and active Services while he has been in the Province, that he has long been desirous of having an opportunity of conferring on you an appointment which might in some respects be more in accordance with your views and wishes.
>
> His Excellency thinks it but due to you to express

> his thanks for your exertions on many occasions in the public Service, and to notice the sacrifices which you have made of your time and health, in carrying on the various duties which you have been entrusted to discharge.
>
> I am also to add that His Excellency will leave a copy of this letter with his Successor, in order that your character and services may be made known to him.[4]

The letter sounded complimentary, but was in effect a brush-off. No doubt Colborne was too concerned about his own future at this crisis in his life to make any special effort on behalf of the clerk of the Assembly. Would he have done so in other circumstances? Not likely, for while Colborne had shown confidence in FitzGibbon by assigning to him numerous responsibilities in fields as varied as law and order, education, public health, customs, and the militia, he had done nothing to assist James in his ambition to rise to the inner circle of the public service. Colborne seemed rather to take so much advantage of FitzGibbon's loyalty and willingness to serve, that the latter became for him an unofficial aide. Even in his final year as lieutenant-governor, Colborne added one more task to FitzGibbon's already multiple duties. He asked the colonel to drill a corps of young men to become officers in the militia. Colborne issued rifles from the military stores for their use. Seventy rifles were available, hence 70 recruits formed the corps. The scheme was part of Colborne's effort to strengthen the militia in case serious disturbances occurred in the future. FitzGibbon was already active as colonel of the Second Regiment, West York Militia, but he took on the assignment, and for three summers trained the recruits twice a week. He received no remuneration, but characteristically went to the personal expense of procuring suitable uniforms for himself and his son Charles, who trained with the corps until he left for Ireland to work with his uncle Henry FitzGibbon, a Dublin businessman. The colonel hoped that the example of himself and his son would encourage the other members of the corps to dress properly in uniform.

An insight into the way Colborne viewed James FitzGibbon is offered in a letter the former wrote to the colonial secretary, Lord John Russell, a few years after he left Upper Canada. The letter was written in connection with a request from FitzGibbon for assistance in obtaining the reward promised him after the Rebellion of 1837. Lord Seaton, as Colborne had become, described FitzGibbon as "an energetic and active Irishman who has long been settled at Toronto, and from his having such influence among his Countrymen has been made use of, and employed by Governors and the local Authorities on every occasion on which firmness and courage were required to restore order in certain Districts".[5] Seaton said nothing of FitzGibbon's long and faithful record of service in his various appointments, nor of the many ways in which he himself had "made use of" FitzGibbon's special talents. One suspects that he betrayed a certain bias when he identified FitzGibbon as an Irishman whose particular usefulness consisted in his influence over other Irishmen, and neglected to mention those numerous services performed by FitzGibbon that had nothing to do with his being Irish.

It is significant that in Upper Canada few Irishmen attained high government positions. In a study of "The Personnel of the Family Compact" by Alison Ewart and Julia Jarvis, of the 36 men they listed as members of the Executive Council from 1791 to 1841, only three — Augustus Baldwin, Peter Russell and R.B. Sullivan — were of Irish origin. Eleven were Canadian and/or of loyalist ancestry, eight were English, seven Scottish, and seven of other or unknown birthplaces. Robert E. Saunders, in his analysis of the Family Compact, named eight men who were at the centre of power in Upper Canada from 1820 to 1837. There was not one Irishman among them.[6] Two of the most distinguished of the Irish in Upper Canada were Dr William Warren Baldwin and his son Robert, but both were noted Reformers opposed to the Tory government. It is impossible to say whether Colborne or his successors might have been more interested in promoting FitzGibbon in the government service if he had been born in England, Scotland or Upper Canada, but there can be no doubt that being born Irish did not enhance his opportunities.

There was one other possible reason for Colborne's failure to obtain preferment for FitzGibbon — there were

Sir Francis Bond Head, Lieutenant-Governor of Upper Canada, 1836-1838

actually very few government posts that paid more than the £360 per annum that FitzGibbon earned (£180 in salary and £180 for special services). Apart from the very highest positions (for which FitzGibbon was not qualified), such as receiver-general, chief justice, or attorney-general, whose salaries were over £1,000, and the judges of the Court of King's Bench who received £900 per year, only seven positions paying £500 or more were listed in the Blue Books of Statistics for Upper Canada in 1836. Some of the more lucrative offices, such as county registrar and district sheriff, paid no salary but were rewarded by fees.

The lieutenant-governor who arrived in Toronto in January 1836 was very different from his predecessors Maitland and Colborne. Short in stature (like William Lyon Mackenzie), with a small head from which a pair of bright blue eyes shone, Sir Francis Bond Head was noted not as a military commander but as the author of entertaining travel books and articles. While employed as a mining supervisor with an English-owned company in Argentina, he had explored the countryside on horseback, describing his travels in lively fashion in a book, *Rough Notes Taken During Some Rapid Journeys Across the Pampas and Among the Andes*. This earned for him the nickname "Galloping Head". But for two years before he came to Upper Canada, Head had served in an entirely different capacity – that of assistant poor law commissioner for the county of Kent in England. He had impressed the British government with his ability as an administrator and conciliator, just what was needed in Upper Canada. His surprising appointment as lieutenant-governor was the result. By his own admission, Head knew nothing of politics or of colonial government. He had never even voted in an election. No one was more surprised than he to be welcomed to Toronto by signs reading "Sir Francis Head, a Tried Reformer", carried by hopeful radicals among the citizens of Toronto who turned out to greet him. The people of Upper Canada soon discovered how misleading those signs were.

After Head's arrival, James FitzGibbon applied for the first position that became available in the higher echelons of the public service, that of surveyor-general of the province. The position was open, not because the incumbent, Samuel Proudfoot Hurd had resigned, but because Lieutenant-Governor Head, after granting Hurd six months' leave of absence on grounds of ill health, immediately replaced him as surveyor-general because of alleged inefficiency, by a man of Head's own choice. Two days later, Head advised his own appointee, Captain J.S. Macaulay, to resign, as he then realized that the appointment was unpopular and that the authority for such an appointment lay not with him. Head had overlooked the usual procedure whereby the lieutenant-governor advised the colonial secretary to appoint a certain candidate for a position; the colonial secretary usually, but not always, acted on that advice.

Among the applicants for the post that became vacant so unexpectedly were James FitzGibbon and John Radenhurst, the clerk in the surveyor-general's department who had worked with FitzGibbon on the La Guayra inquiry. FitzGibbon addressed his application to Head's secretary, John Joseph. It was an unpleasing mixture of pride and humility. With pride, he stated that, "an ardent zeal for that Service in which I have been raised from a very humble rank to a respectable elevation has carried me along on every occasion where I thought I could do honor to The King's Government or advance its interests". This positive statement was nullified by the humble one that followed: "Much as my circumstances may induce me to ask for this appointment with more than ordinary earnestness, yet I request that I may not be considered as an applicant if a more eligible candidate shall be brought under His Excellency's consideration". As to his qualifications for the position, FitzGibbon had nothing specific to offer beyond saying, "On my general Knowledge of business, on my activity and application, and on the Knowledge I already possess of the affairs of that Department I rest my hopes of being able efficiently to discharge the duties of Surveyor General".[7] It was not an impressive application, and was passed over. Although Radenhurst's application was supported by some prominent people, Head rejected it, wisely, because of Radenhurst's involvement in private land deals.

The appointment was not made for several months, and then it went to a non-applicant, John Macaulay of Kingston, who had been recommended to Head by William Allan. The latter knew Macaulay through his connection with the Bank of Upper Canada, of which Allan was president for several years and Macaulay its Kingston agent. More recently, the two had shared membership in the Legislative Council. The choice of Macaulay as surveyor-general illustrated the way in which appointees for government posts were frequently selected in Upper Canada. In addition to being recommended by a member of the Family Compact, John Macaulay, like George Markland in a former case, was of loyalist descent and, like Markland, had attended John Strachan's school and was a friend of John Beverley Robinson.

Macaulay also had experience and ability that qualified him for a high government post. Besides his position in the Bank of Upper Canada, he had served as postmaster at Kingston, justice of the peace, secretary to the customs duty commission and since January 1836 as Legislative Councillor. By comparison, James FitzGibbon had few qualifications for the post of surveyor-general, as to judge by the apologetic tone of his application, he himself recognized.

FitzGibbon withdrew from the competition some months before Macaulay's appointment was made. Perhaps he did so because of the peculiar circumstances surrounding the vacancy. At any rate, FitzGibbon adopted a new approach. He tried to win the interest and favour of Lieutenant-Governor Head by addressing a memorial to him. This was a long biographical letter in which FitzGibbon outlined his career in the military and public services; made his customary explanation about his debts (then £2,000) and his consequent need for an increase in income; described in detail his work during the cholera epidemic; and told how he had quelled the two York riots. He threatened to resign from the militia, the magistracy and other special services for which, he said, he had received no "relief or advantage" in the past. He apologized for writing about his past services at such length, saying that he had no other way of making them known to the lieutenant-governor, as "he never served a party for party purposes .... No party therefore has a special interest in laying before Your Excellency his claims". In his covering letter to Head's secretary, FitzGibbon stressed his habit of self-reliance: "Upon my own efforts to serve the Public I have ever relied for the patronage of the Government, and not upon Individual Patrons, on whom I might rely for stating my services to the Head of the Government".[8] This was a reference to the direct relationship he had enjoyed with both Maitland and Colborne. Now he realized that he was facing a new situation in which he suffered under the handicap of having no powerful friend within the circle of government advisers. It was not enough to have talent, zeal and a record of faithful service in order to obtain preferment; one must also have the right patron to plead one's cause and, argued FitzGibbon, one must serve the right political party. As clerk of the Assembly FitzGibbon could hardly be an active party supporter, although no one could have had any doubts about where his sympathies lay. His memorial failed in its objective, but he did not resign from any of his offices.

Soon Head called upon James FitzGibbon to perform the kind of service for which he was noted – the quelling of riots. Trouble had arisen at the Cornwall Canal, which was being built to bypass the Long Sault in the St Lawrence. As in the earlier outbreak near Perth, fighting had erupted between the Irish, in this case the workers on the canal, and the established settlers. As before, there was a call for troops. The spokesman for the community was Archibald McLean, a prominent lawyer in Cornwall, a justice of the peace, speaker of the House of Assembly, and a member of the Legislative Council. His letter to Lieutenant-Governor Head arrived in the midst of the 1836 election campaign, in which McLean was a candidate and Head was an active campaigner. Head had dissolved the House of Assembly following obstruction by the Reformers, and he had then gone out speaking on behalf of the Constitutionalists (the conservatives) contrary to the usual practice of non-participation by governors during an election. McLean's request for troops presented Head with a dilemma. He could not overlook the serious situation described by this highly respected official, who told of outrages committed by the canal workmen, of retaliation by the inhabitants, of vengeance threatened by the workmen, and possible violence during the election. At the same time, Head did not wish to be accused of intimidation while the election campaign was in progress. He turned to FitzGibbon to save the situation, just as Maitland had done, 12 years previously.

The lieutenant-governor "commanded" Colonel FitzGibbon to go to Cornwall, there to consult with Mr McLean and the other magistrates, and "to see the Canal labourers, from whom the danger seems to be apprehended, to the end that by every means of persuasion in your power, you may induce them to refer their quarrel to the legal tribunals of the Country". As a precaution, FitzGibbon was to take with him, from Kingston, 50 stand of arms along with ammunition, which he was to deliver to the magistrates at Cornwall only if he should find that the use of arms was necessary. And so that FitzGibbon might have adequate authority, Head appointed him a justice of the peace for the Eastern District.[9]

This was a much tougher assignment than FitzGibbon had faced in the Bathurst District. There he had acted as mediator between two groups of angry settlers whose basic wish was to farm peaceably. On the Cornwall Canal, he had to deal with hundreds of unruly Irish labourers who were living in huts and lacked the restraints of family life. Two murders committed by canal workers had raised the fears of the local inhabitants, many of whom were descended from Loyalists of German or Dutch origin. The most recent murder had occurred early in 1836 when two canal workers had brutally beaten a prominent landowner, Albert French, after he refused to give them and their female companion a ride. The three had driven off in French's sleigh leaving him dying in the snow. The murderers had been arrested. One later escaped but the other, Michael Connell, was in the Cornwall jail awaiting trial.

The "outrages" to which Archibald McLean referred had come later, following a violent fight that had taken place at the entrance to a show put on by a travelling menagerie (lions, tigers, elephants, zebras and other wild animals) not far from the Long Sault. A woman had slipped through the gates without paying, and the gateman had mistakenly ejected the wife of a canal workman, who in fact had paid her way. This sparked a fight between the canal workers and the circus men assisted by some spectators. The Irish canalmen won that fight, but the others immediately armed themselves with weapons, waylaid the workers on a narrow bridge on their way home from the show, and beat them savagely. Since then, according to McLean, the inhabitants had been afraid to travel on the public highway for fear of being attacked and beaten by the revengeful canalmen.

James FitzGibbon went into this dangerous situation with his customary courage. He travelled by steamboat (except for the necessary portage by wagon between Dickinson's Landing and Cornwall), stopping at Kingston en route to pick up the arms and ammunition. On his arrival at Cornwall on Friday 24 June he wasted no time, but rode that afternoon for several kilometres along the canal in company with the supervising engineer, Captain George Phillpotts. This was the first of his daily rides. He learned on the first afternoon that the violence had been confined to the Long Sault end of the canal. The contractors at the Cornwall end had the first choice of workers, hence the less desirable ones were filtered out and drifted along the canal towards the western end.

In an astute move, FitzGibbon invited the assistance of the local priest, the Reverend James P. Bennet, and on Saturday the two of them, accompanied by the sheriff (who was also a Roman Catholic), rode the full length of the canal. The priest spoke more favourably of the canal workers than anyone else had, and FitzGibbon learned also from "impartial persons" that the country people and the menagerie showmen, who had attacked the canalmen on the bridge, had "behaved with great cruelty to those they overtook by beating them inhumanly with heavy clubs and the Iron Bars taken from the cages of the Wild Beasts". In retaliation, the canal workers had pulled three people off their horses, two days later, but had committed no other violence, though false reports of assaults continued to be circulated. Rumours were spread that one political party was trying to induce canal workers to intimidate voters at the polls in the coming election, and again, that the other political party was doing the same. Such intimidation was not unusual in those days of open voting, but as the number of workers on the canal had increased to about 3,000, FitzGibbon feared that a "most formidable" situation might develop if they chose to create disturbances on the two election days.[10] The voting was to take place in Cornwall on two days: Saturday 2 July for the county member, and Monday, the fourth, for the town.

It was rumoured that on the Roman Catholic holiday of St Peter and St Paul's Day, 29 June, the men from the Long Sault would go to Cornwall and perhaps try to release the accused murderer Michael Connell. FitzGibbon consulted the Eastern District magistrates and the Board of Police. He distributed the boxes of arms that he had brought from Kingston but left them unpacked. Six reliable men were stationed in the jail on the day of the holiday and were left on duty all night. FitzGibbon requested Father Bennet to celebrate the holiday mass with the canal workers at the Long Sault instead of at Cornwall, thus heading off any necessity for the men to go into town. He himself rode out to the Long Sault accompanied by the canal agent, William R.F. Burford. The precautions proved successful: no difficulties arose. In the evening, Father Bennet rode back into town with the other two men, who watched in amazement as the priest wielded his influence over the workers in a manner that was far from spiritual. When a number of the men were seen to be drunk and fighting, "the Priest immediately rode through between them and with his Whip dispersed them instantly. He then dismounted and entered the Tavern where many others were drinking, whence he expelled them thro' the Windows and Doors, and on coming out he called from a distance a number of sober men and made them convey the drunken men to their several Huts".

The streets were quiet in Cornwall that evening, but it was reported that two Irishmen had been overheard saying that Irish prisoners in the jail would be freed that night. Consequently FitzGibbon decided to join the six trustworthy men in the Cornwall jail. "The night passed quietly and I left the Gaol at 4 this morning", he reported the next day.[11]

On the first election day FitzGibbon again rode out to the Long Sault, accompanied this time by Captain Phillpotts. They heard reports that some men had stopped work and that others had been incited to go into Cornwall. In the end, all the men were persuaded to stay on the job. The polls were supposed to remain open until 7 p.m., but as FitzGibbon and Phillpotts approached Cornwall on their ride back in the middle of the afternoon, they met the voters returning from town. The election was over and Alexander McLean had been declared winner. There had been no more than the usual fighting at the polls. The second election day passed peaceably, and FitzGibbon left Cornwall the next day.

While travelling to Toronto on the steamer *Great Britain*, FitzGibbon prepared his final report to John Joseph. He recommended that a company of one of the regular regiments be transferred to Cornwall for the time being. He reasoned that if local troops such as the militia were relied upon to put down riots or enforce the law, the canal workers in resentment "would threaten the lives and property of those who would be most active against them". Some of the local people, on their part, had already threatened to turn out *en masse* to exterminate the workmen if they continued to cause trouble, FitzGibbon said. "Therefore to overawe the turbulently disposed on both sides, and to give confidence to those who love peace", he recommended that regular troops be stationed at Cornwall until the canal was finished or until the threat of violence came to an end.[12]

FitzGibbon's advice was followed. A company of the 15th Regiment was ordered from Kingston to Cornwall, where it remained about two months. It was feared that disturbances might erupt at the time of Michael Connell's trial and subsequent execution in August, but nothing of the sort happened and the troops were withdrawn soon after.

Once again James FitzGibbon had demonstrated his exceptional skill in restoring peace in violent situations. At Cornwall, as in the Bathurst District, his natural sympathy for the Irish newcomers (the underdogs and the accused), combined with his ability to listen to both sides in the quarrel and to work with local officials, helped calm the atmosphere and inspire confidence in him as conciliator. Contributing enormously to his skill were his personal characteristics: his wit and good humour, his courage and his impressive physique, plus his willingness to give unstintingly of his time and energy, to the point of exhaustion.

FitzGibbon had saved Lieutenant-Governor Head from embarrassment during the election, which the Tories won by a large majority, yet Head did not reward him with a promotion. The qualities that FitzGibbon displayed were not the kind that impressed Sir Francis, who liked greater flamboyance, such as that of Allan MacNab, the Hamilton member of the Legislative Assembly and afterwards its speaker, who became a great favourite of Head's.

Some months after his Cornwall assignment, FitzGibbon appealed again to the lieutenant-governor to consider his case, and again he stressed his lack of party connections. "The services which I have rendered to this Government were not rendered in alliance with any political party in the Province, but for the general good", he said. "No party, therefore, feels or takes special interest in my advancement or prosperity". He sounded a note of cynicism and despair as he wrote of the pressure exerted on government officials by their relatives and friends who sought advancement, and he suggested that, contrariwise, some of Head's advisers worked against him.

> I do not expect that my claims will be urged by any one to be taken into Your Excellency's consideration. But on the contrary, were my name mentioned, I apprehend it would be received coldly by some of those around Your Excellency; and although no one may venture to hazard a direct objection to me, yet I and my claims may be depreciated by faint praise as effectually as if I were really undeserving. The eagerness of interested men to procure elevation for their Relatives or attached political supporters must cause them to exercise their most ingenious faculties to attain success. It is easy to hint or to insinuate that I am without scholastic education — of low origin — and that I do not possess property, acquirements or manners to fit me for the duties or society of men in the higher offices

Anna Brownell Jameson, author of Winter Studies and Summer Rambles in Canada *(1838)*

of the Government.

I admit that all I know has been gleaned by me in the great school of the World; yet if an unerring scale of comparative merits be applied to men I would not decline to place myself among those who are likely to be candidates for the higher offices of this Government, where professional qualifications are not indispensible [*sic*].[13]

FitzGibbon ended his letter by saying that he looked to his Excellency alone for favourable consideration – a vain hope that Head would step into the breach of patronage left by the departure of Colborne.

A shrewd observer of the Upper Canadian scene arrived in Toronto in December 1836 and remained in the province nine months. This was Anna Brownell Jameson, wife of Robert S. Jameson, then attorney-general of Upper Canada. Mrs Jameson took a fancy to Colonel FitzGibbon, saying that, "The men who have interested me through life were all self-educated, and what are called originals. This dear, good F. is *originalissimo*". FitzGibbon amused Mrs Jameson, who was also Irish-born, with stories of his boyhood in Ireland and of his life in the army, and he told her of his romantic marriage. "With so much overflowing benevolence and fearless energy of character, and all the eccentricity, and sensibility, and poetry, and headlong courage of his country, you cannot wonder that this brave and worthy man interests me", she wrote.

Mrs Jameson viewed the political scene in Upper Canada with insight. "We have here", she wrote, "a petty colonial oligarchy, a self-constituted aristocracy, based upon nothing real, nor even upon any thing imaginary". She sensed that the mood in the province was resentful, that the Upper Canadians suffered from "the total absence of all sympathy on the part of the English government with the condition, the wants, the feelings, the capabilities of the people and country".[14] Mrs Jameson left Canada three months before the outbreak of rebellion.

As the signs of revolt increased, James FitzGibbon

became alarmed, but when he tried to warn Lieutenant-Governor Head he was met by incredulity and irritation. In the days immediately preceding the uprising, James FitzGibbon faced one of the greatest crises of his life.

Chapter Seven

The Colonel Leads the Attack Against the Rebels

The election of July 1836 struck a shattering blow to the Reformers. Their numbers were reduced to a third of the Assembly, and William Lyon Mackenzie was defeated for the first time since he had entered politics. He was so mortified when he heard the news, said his son-in-law Charles Lindsey, that he retired with a few supporters to the house of a friend and "wept like a child". Several of his friends wept with him.[1] Lieutenant-Governor Head had campaigned vigorously for the Constitutionalist party, declaring that it stood for loyalty to the British connection. Head's simple but forceful message played especially upon the fears of recent British immigrants who wanted, above all, to maintain their link with Great Britain. There were, of course, other factors that affected the election results: concern over the deteriorating economy, the surprising union of Orange and Roman Catholic forces to fight the Reformers, and the change in voting practices of many Methodists, who switched from the Reformers to the Tories in this election.

Mackenzie returned to journalism. He had given up the *Colonial Advocate* the previous year, but now launched a new paper, *The Constitution*, to provide a voice for the dissidents and an invitation to revolt.

The radicals were not the only ones discouraged by the outcome of the election. The moderate Reformers, such as Robert Baldwin, were also disheartened. Baldwin

James FitzGibbon, Acting Adjutant-General of Militia, Upper Canada, December 1837

had gone to England before the election hoping to see Colonial Secretary Lord Glenelg and warn him of the dangerous situation that was developing in Upper Canada. When he failed to obtain an interview, he submitted a memorandum to Lord Glenelg, setting forth his ideas on how responsible government should function in Upper Canada. (This paper may have influenced Lord Durham when he made his report in 1839). After the election, Robert Baldwin resumed his law practice in Toronto and did not return to politics until after the Act of Union.

At first, all went peacefully in the new provincial Assembly, but the tranquility was short-lived. Sir Francis Bond Head, triumphant in victory, seemed blissfully unaware of the storm signals. "Upon the Loyalty of the People of Upper Canada his Majesty's Government may now build as upon a Rock", he wrote in a memorandum to the colonial secretary.[2] Head refused to make any conciliatory gesture towards the Reformers and he rejected the advice of Lord Glenelg about certain government appointments. His relations with his superiors in London speedily declined.

Spring of 1837 ushered in a financial crisis and an economic depression. Upper Canada, with its small population of about 400,000, was adversely affected by the business slump in the United States. Business failures in the province, unemployment, and hard times in farming areas caused discontent among the settlers. In the neighbouring province of Lower Canada, the rift between the people and the government was widening, and the drift towards rebellion gained momentum. The radical Reformers of Toronto drew up a declaration outlining their complaints against the government, expressing their thanks to Louis Joseph Papineau, leader of the *Patriotes* of Lower Canada, for showing them the way, and urging the Reformers of Upper Canada to make common cause with their fellow citizens of the lower province. The declaration appeared in *The Constitution* of 2 August 1837, and the radicals set up a Committee of Vigilance with Mackenzie as agent and corresponding secretary.

The rebellious Reformers began holding meetings in villages and rural centres north and west of Toronto. *The Constitution* of 23 August 1837 reported that 300 attended a meeting in Newmarket, 400 in Lloydtown, 300 in Trafalgar, 90 in Caledon, 127 in Esquesing, and so on. These numbers may have been exaggerated, and some who attended the meetings were not so much rebellious as curious. On occasion, the Tories were numerous enough to take charge and to pass resolutions expressing loyalty to the Queen and the lieutenant-governor. Nevertheless the meetings continued to draw crowds of dissatisfied settlers, many of whom were American-born and lacked the strong sense of British loyalty that characterized the United Empire Loyalists and the recent British immigrants. Usually at the meetings, Mackenzie spoke, someone read the Toronto "declaration of independence", and the assembled radicals appointed a local vigilance committee. Sometimes the Orangemen and other opponents caused disruptions that led to bloody skirmishes and in self-defence the rebels began arming themselves with hickory sticks, pikes and rifles. They began drilling with muskets and rifles, holding target practices and "turkey shoots". The ill-fated blacksmith of Holland Landing, Samuel Lount, forged pike-heads and cast bullets in his shop.

Rumours reached Toronto of the drilling and target practice. Reports of the local meetings appeared in the Tory *Patriot* as well as Mackenzie's *Constitution*, yet the lieutenant-governor refused to be alarmed. When Colborne, as commander-in-chief of the armed forces in the two Canadas, wrote to Head in October 1837 asking that troops be sent from Upper Canada to supplement those in Lower Canada, Head responded by sending all the troops requested, and insisted on sending as well the two detachments that remained. He explained to Colborne that he wanted to prove to the people in England, "that this Province requires no Troops at all, and consequently that it is *perfectly tranquil*".[3] When he ordered the final detachment of the 24th Regiment to proceed from Penetanguishene to Montreal, Colonel James FitzGibbon became alarmed. "On its approach to Toronto", he wrote, "I ventured to advise His Excellency to detain it here, but he said he would not keep a Soldier in the Province".

At first, like other government officials, FitzGibbon was not worried by reports that the radicals were drilling. He thought their purpose was to alarm the government and thus inhibit it from sending more assistance to Lower Canada to help put down the rebels in that province. "I did not then think any considerable portion of the disaffected in Upper Canada would peril their all on the risk of Rebellion", he said in his "Narrative of Occurrences" written shortly after the rebellion took place. "But as November advanced", FitzGibbon continued, "I became day by day more impressed with an apprehension that the peace of the Province would be disturbed".[4] When a quantity of arms (2500 muskets with bayonets, 500 rifles and ammunition) was sent from Kingston to Toronto, Head ordered that the arms be stored in the market building under the protection of the city authorities rather than of the militia, in order to prevent the appearance of coercion. Two constables stood guard over the arms and ammunition at night. FitzGibbon considered this protection inadequate. He feared that the rebels would come into the city one by one, hide with their friends and then converge at night on the City Hall (the market building), and take possession of it and of the military supplies. (Mackenzie actually did try to persuade his fellow conspirators, soon after the troops left the province, to take Government House by surprise, seize the lieutenant-governor, imprison him at City Hall, and capture the munitions so badly needed by the rebels, but his more cautious colleagues would not agree to the plan).

FitzGibbon proposed to Head that some of the specially trained riflemen of his volunteer militia corps act as a guard at City Hall and furnish sentries for Government House, but Head "quickly, and even pettishly refused", saying that he had instead considered moving the arms from City Hall to Government House and placing them in the care of his domestic servants. Then he asked FitzGibbon to put his offer in writing. The next day FitzGibbon was surprised to see his letter published in *The Patriot.* "It was now plain to me", FitzGibbon wrote afterwards, that "His Excellency desired to be urged to take measures of defence, that he might show forth to the Province that he had no fear of rebellion, . . . I am convinced that His Excellency was confident he could keep all in peace and safety, with his own Goose Quill".[5]

The lieutenant-governor recieved support for his

complaisant attitude from Chief Justice John Beverley Robinson, who wrote privately to him on the first of November 1837, saying:

> I have heard whispers in two or three quarters ab't preparations, & militia movements, volunteering &c. I fear this is all mischievous in sev'l points of view, our true strength in my opinion is to be perfectly quiet . . . . I should as soon expect the farmers of Buckinghamshire to march in & attack the tower as the farmers of a few back townships of this Dis't to make any movement ag't this town.[6]

Surveyor-General John Macaulay was more apprehensive. His alarm was shared by Egerton Ryerson, the prominent Methodist minister and editor of the *Christian Guardian*, who observed that men were assembling at clandestine meetings and were being drilled in the use of weapons. "I pressed upon Sir Francis the propriety and importance of making some prudent provision for the defence of the city, in case any party should be urged on in the madness of rebellion so far as to attack it", Ryerson wrote to a friend after the insurrection had begun.[7]

About the middle of November, Sir John Colborne reported that the French-speaking population of Lower Canada was uniting against the government, and asked Head to send militia reinforcements. He suggested that a number of militia companies might be stationed on guard at certain points in the lower province. Perversely, and in striking contrast to his previous action in sending Colborne more troops than he had requested, Head refused to move any of the militia. He was aware of the situation in Lower Canada, and he wrote to Colborne that the agitators were trying to create disturbances in Upper Canada as well, but he himself refused to be agitated. In sending all his troops to Lower Canada he had presented a challenge to the rebels, and the manoeuvre had worked. The rebels had taken no action. The present political state of the province was entirely satisfactory, he assured Colborne, and he wished to leave it that way.

Notwithstanding the lieutenant-governor's confidence that all was well, the rebels of Upper Canada continued their preparations for revolt. Mackenzie published a draft constitution for the future state. Two weeks later, he distributed a handbill headed "Independence!" and calling on "brave Canadians", in the cause of freedom, to "Get ready your rifles, and make short work of it".[8] The drilling of men and the manufacture of pike-heads continued.

Colonel FitzGibbon's fear of armed insurrection increased, and he determined to take some steps himself against a possible attack on Toronto. FitzGibbon compiled a list of those men who lived west of Yonge Street on whose loyalty he could depend. He meant to call on them individually, warn them of the danger, and ask them to sleep with their guns loaded and their clothes handy, so they could quickly assemble at the Parliament Building if they heard the bell of Upper Canada College ringing the alarm. The colonel himself would see that the bell was rung in case of crisis. He proposed asking Mayor George Gurnett to warn similarly the loyal citizens living east of Yonge and to instruct them to assemble at City Hall if they should hear the church bells ringing.

FitzGibbon called on the lieutenant-governor with his list of 126 names and explained his plan. While Head looked over the list, Colonel FitzGibbon said, with uncharacteristic defiance:

> For the doing of this I desire to have your Excellency's sanction, but permit me to tell Your Excellency that whether you give me leave or not I am determined to do it . . . . I say so with all due respect to Your Excellency, as the Representative of my Sovereign; but you are so convinced that we are in no danger, that you will take no measure of precaution; but I, being fully convinced that the danger is most imminent, am determined to take every measure in my power to devise for the protection of my family and friends.

Sir Francis looked at FitzGibbon "with an expression of surprise, or anger, on his face", but after he had read the list he said, unexpectedly, "Well I think this is a good measure, and you have my sanction for carrying it out".[9]

The next step was to enlist the support of the mayor. FitzGibbon went to see him and he appeared to acquiesce, but when the crisis came a few days later, he took no

St. James Anglican Church, Toronto, as in 1833-1849

action, regarding FitzGibbon's conduct as officious interference. Others besides Gurnett were irritated by FitzGibbon, whom they saw as a disturbing fanatic. When the colonel visited Chief Justice Robinson during his round of calls on the citizens west of Yonge Street, Robinson rebuked him for alarming the people. (As it turned out, FitzGibbon had time to warn only 50 people on his list before the crisis occurred).

Reports reached Toronto at the end of November that the *Patriotes* of Lower Canada had defeated the British troops at St Denis. The news spurred the Upper Canadian rebels and disturbed the complacency of government officials. On Saturday 2 December a number of officials met at Government House to consider the situation. They concluded that the idea of revolt in Upper Canada was too ridiculous to merit serious attention. Comfortably ensconced in power, strongly supported by the United Empire Loyalists and the recent British settlers, the leaders of the government circle were sheltered from the winds of dissension and change. But even while they were reassuring themselves, FitzGibbon was hearing a very different story. An unexpected visitor, a mysterious Mr "L", came to see him in his office in the Parliament Building and insisted on speaking to him alone. They went into the speaker's room for privacy, and there Mr "L" disclosed that he had observed preparations being made in his neighbourhood north of Toronto that pointed to an armed uprising. He had seen bags in the blacksmith shop filled with what he believed were pike-heads, and long wooden handles said to be for pitchforks or rakes but which he surmised were pike-handles. FitzGibbon urged Mr "L" to go with him to Government House to report his information but the man hesitated for fear his rebel neighbours should discover that he had informed on them. He confided in FitzGibbon as a fellow Mason and former deputy provincial grand master, and therefore someone to be trusted.

Who was this Mr "L"? It is known only that he was a magistrate from somewhere north of Toronto. Probably he was William Laughton, a magistrate of Holland Landing. Laughton was a prosperous businessman (in later years he owned a steamer that plied on Lake Simcoe), and he lived near Samuel Lount's blacksmith shop. After the rebellion he was a witness in the indictment against Samuel Lount's brother George, who was charged with treason.[10]

Mr "L" finally agreed to go to Government House if the lieutenant-governor should insist upon seeing him, but first he urged Colonel FitzGibbon to go by himself and deliver the message. On his arrival the colonel was shown into the room where the government officials were assembled. Seated with the lieutenant-governor were Chief Justice Robinson, Christopher Hagerman (who had succeeded Robert Jameson as attorney-general), Solicitor-General William Henry Draper, Speaker Allan MacNab, and two Executive Councillors – R.B. Sullivan and William Allan. As might be expected, the officials were not impressed by FitzGibbon's information; they asked, however, to see the man who had brought the alarming report. Mr "L" was sent for, and meanwhile the discussion resumed on the state of the province. FitzGibbon related afterwards that

> No one present appeared to have any apprehension of approaching danger. I expressed mine very strongly, and from time to time urged upon His Excellency the necessity of arming in our defence. Upon one occasion, Judge [Jonas] Jones, who sat next to me on my right hand, turned towards me and said, "You do not mean to say that these people are going to rebel"? To which I answered "Most distinctly I do, sir". Whereupon he turned from me towards his Excellency and exclaimed, most contemptuously, "Pugh! Pugh!"[11]

Jones' contempt was intended, no doubt, for the messenger as much as for the message. To Mr Justice Jones, FitzGibbon was an alarmist of little more consequence than a buzzing mosquito. He was also an intruder. Jonas Jones was a proud member of the Family Compact by virtue of his family (he was the son of Ephraim Jones who had acted as commissary for the first group of Loyalists that arrived in Grenville county in 1784), his education (a pupil of John Strachan), his friends from school days (John Beverley Robinson, John Macaulay and George Markland), and his own achievement as one of the early lawyers admitted to the Bar of Upper Canada, and now puisne judge of the Court of King's Bench.

Mr "L" arrived at Government House and he was shown into an adjoining room. There he was questioned by Sir Francis Head and Attorney-General Hagerman. Afterwards, Hagerman said, "Why the information brought by this Magistrate is at third or fourth hand and does not at all make the same impression as what Col. FitzGibbon said". FitzGibbon protested, "Not at fourth hand, Sir, but what impression has it made on Mr "L" 's own mind"? At this point, the Honourable William Allan, a pragmatic Scot, came to FitzGibbon's support, saying, "Gentlemen, do you expect the Rebels will come and give you information of their doings at first hand? . . . I concur in every word Col. FitzGibbon has said and think that not a moment should be lost in making preparations to meet the approaching danger". The other officials remained obstinate. Lieutenant-Governor Head said, "I hold the same opinion I always held, that there is no danger whatever", but he suggested that if the magistrates and inhabitants of Toronto were apprehensive of danger, they should address an appeal to him. It so happened that Mayor Gurnett, who had become disturbed by the rumours, was even then waiting in another room for an interview with Sir Francis.

Before FitzGibbon withdrew, he made one more appeal for defensive action. He urged Head to summon the half-pay officers and veterans of the city to man the garrison. Head refused: "What will the people of England say if they hear that we are thus arming"? and he suggested that such a step might offend the militia. The lieutenant-governor's pride was at stake. Having adopted a policy wrongly based on implicit faith in the loyalty of the people, he could not agree now to armed preparations. "From the whole tenor of His Excellency's observations", FitzGibbon wrote afterwards, "it was plain to me that he had it entirely at heart to prove to the Government and People of Britain that he could preserve Upper Canada in tranquility during the winter by his own management, without a single soldier, or a step being taken to guard against or to prevent disturbance".[12]

Despite the firm stand taken by Head on Saturday,

by Monday he had changed his position, whether persuaded by FitzGibbon's arguments, or by William Allan or Mayor Gurnett, or by additional information. That morning, 4 December, he summoned Colonel FitzGibbon to Government House and appointed him acting adjutant-general of militia. (Nathaniel Coffin was still the adjutant-general, but he was over 70, ill and incompetent, and he had petitioned the lieutenant-governor, six months previously, to permit him to retire on salary). Head then issued a general order requesting the militia regiments of Upper Canada to prepare for service.

The militia order had to be printed and could not be ready for circulation to the militia officers until the next day. The colonel became extremely apprehensive, and on the afternoon of that same Monday returned to Government House to renew his pressure on the lieutenant-governor to organize the half-pay officers and discharged soldiers in defence of the garrison. This time Head gave his consent, but it was too late in the day to act on the decision. FitzGibbon remained tense and worried, and feared that he was a marked man. He recollected that Mackenzie had recently commented on his volunteer rifle corps in *The Constitution*. FitzGibbon decided that it would be risky to sleep at home and he would spend the night in his office in the Parliament Building. He invited some loyal friends to share the vigil with him. About 20 came, bearing arms. They found the colonel full of foreboding.

In the meantime, confusion reigned among the rebels. They had set Thursday 7 December for their advance on Toronto. They intended to assemble secretly at Montgomery's Tavern on Yonge Street, six kilometres north of Toronto (just north of present-day Eglinton Avenue), march to the city under the command of Colonel Anthony Van Egmond, a veteran officer who had served under Napoleon and who lived in the Huron Tract, take possession of City Hall and the munitions stored there, imprison Lieutenant-Governor Head, and with the help of friends inside the city, take over the government. Dr John Rolph, the crafty, enigmatic but highly intelligent Reformer, was to manage the revolt (the details to be worked out by Mackenzie), and afterwards act as administrator of the provisional government. (Some historians doubt that Rolph was to direct the operations of the uprising itself but it is certain that Mackenzie consulted Rolph, and that Rolph was advised of the date on which the rebel forces were to assemble).

On the Saturday on which FitzGibbon received the visit from the mysterious Mr "L", Dr Rolph heard rumours that the government was taking precautionary measures and intended to arrest Mackenzie. These rumours probably sprang from observations that government officials were meeting at Government House. Dr Rolph decided to advance the date for their march on Toronto to Monday, the fourth of December. He sent word to Samuel Lount, the American-born blacksmith who was a key leader of the rebellion. Two of the other main participants were the farmer-surveyor David Gibson, who was a member of the House of Assembly, and Anthony Anderson, a militia captain of Lloydtown, who with the exception of Van Egmond was the most experienced military leader. Lount and Anderson, acting on Rolph's advice, notified their men to prepare to assemble at Montgomery's Tavern on Monday instead of Thursday. Mackenzie, who was somewhere in the country north of Toronto, did not learn of the change of plan until Sunday night. The news astonished him. He was very angry and tried to countermand the order, but it was too late; some of the men were already on their way to Montgomery's. The next day Mackenzie held a private meeting in a farmhouse with Dr Rolph, who had by that time concluded that the planned attack on Toronto should be called off. That was impossible Mackenzie told him; things had gone too far.

On Monday evening the men who arrived at Montgomery's Tavern were in no condition to advance on Toronto. They were tired from their long march; many of them were hungry but food was lacking at the tavern; moreover, the promised arms had failed to materialize. Most of the men were armed only with pikes; a few had rifles. The rebel leaders finally decided that in lieu of the intended march on Toronto, a party of four would ride down Yonge Street to the city on a scouting expedition. Mackenzie, Anderson, Joseph Shepard and Robert Smith formed the party.

William Lyon Mackenzie

While Mackenzie and his companions set out from the tavern, the restless Colonel FitzGibbon called once again at Government House to warn Sir Francis of the danger he anticipated. The lieutenant-governor had gone to bed early, but FitzGibbon insisted on seeing him. Head soon appeared, in his dressing-gown. His temper was not improved when he heard FitzGibbon say that he "apprehended some outbreak would take place that very night". Head was unimpressed. He went back to bed and the colonel returned to his quarters in the Parliament Building. Within an hour, someone brought word that the rebels were assembling at Montgomery's Tavern and that they planned to march on Toronto that night. FitzGibbon borrowed a horse from the Parliament House messenger so he could ride up Yonge Street and see for himself. But first, he rode to the houses of the principal men who lived west of Yonge, warning them of the rebels' approach and instructing them to go at once to the Parliament Building or to City Hall. Again he interrupted the lieutenant-governor's sleep and again His Excellency refused to be alarmed. He retired to bed as before. Others too were disbelieving. When a man sent by FitzGibbon called on Judge Jonas Jones, the latter responded angrily: "What is all this noise about? Who desired you to call me"? The messenger replied that FitzGibbon had sent him, whereupon Jones exclaimed, "Oh! the over zeal of that man is giving us a great deal of trouble".[13]

FitzGibbon sent a young law student, John Hillyard Cameron (afterwards a well-known lawyer prominent in the Tory party) to ring the bell at Upper Canada College. This was to be the cue for Mayor Gurnett to set the church bells ringing, but he did nothing. In desperation, FitzGibbon himself went to St James Church. He found it locked, sent someone for the key, and soon he had the bells ringing out their warning to all the citizens of Toronto. Next, the colonel gave directions for the cases of arms in City Hall to be opened and the weapons distributed to volunteers as they came in.

At last, FitzGibbon mounted his horse and rode up Yonge Street, accompanied by two law students from his volunteer rifle corps: George Brock and William Bellingham. (Brock was a cousin of the late Sir Isaac

Brock and the son of a former fellow officer in the 49th Regiment). The three men rode as far as the ravine on Yonge Street where Sheriff William Botsford Jarvis lived in his house "Rosedale". They failed to see any sign of the rebels, and FitzGibbon began to wonder if the report had been false. He felt he might be better employed in Toronto organizing the volunteers, but he was anxious to know what was happening at Montgomery's. Brock and Bellingham volunteered to ride on and find out, and FitzGibbon turned back towards the city. The two young men had gone only a couple of hundred metres when they were taken prisoner by the rebels.

As Colonel FitzGibbon rode back to Toronto he saw two horsemen approaching. They were Alderman John Powell (soon to be mayor) and Archibald McDonald, a wharfinger. Like FitzGibbon, these men had decided to ride north and reconnoitre. FitzGibbon urged them to hasten and try to overtake Brock and Bellingham. The men rode on. After a short distance they were accosted by Mackenzie and his three fellow rebels. Mackenzie recognized Powell and McDonald. He drew out his double-barrelled pistol, asked several questions about the situation in Toronto and then told the men they would have to go to Montgomery's Tavern as prisoners. Mackenzie's account of this episode differs from John Powell's in some details but both agree that Anderson and Shepard were assigned to escort Powell and McDonald to the rebel camp while Mackenzie and Smith continued on their way towards Toronto. As the party with the prisoners rode north they met a horseman who told them that Lieutenant-Colonel Robert Moodie, a half-pay army officer and veteran of the War of 1812, had been shot at Montgomery's Tavern. This news alarmed Powell and his companion. When the party was approaching its destination, Powell managed to get slightly behind Anderson and, drawing his pistol, shot his captor in the back of the neck. Anderson fell to the ground, dead. Powell and McDonald swung their horses around and galloped back down Yonge Street. Shepard fired at them but missed. When the two fugitives passed Mackenzie, McDonald well in the lead, Mackenzie and Smith pursued them. Mackenzie fired at Powell over his horse's head. Powell then slackened his pace, let Mackenzie come alongside him and, in Mackenzie's words, "*suddenly clapt a pistol quite close to my right breast*, but the priming flashed in the pan, and thus I was saved from instant death". Powell galloped off. McDonald was soon captured and Smith accompanied him back to Montgomery's.

The rebel leader was now alone on Yonge Street and he "judged it most prudent to return to Montgomery's". He was shocked to find Anderson's body on the road; this was his first clue as to how Powell and McDonald had escaped. When he got back to the tavern, he learned that Colonel Moodie had been seriously wounded as he tried to charge past the guard on his way to Toronto from Richmond Hill. Moodie was cared for at the tavern but he died a few hours later.

Meanwhile, John Powell, galloping hard to reach the city, thought he heard his pursuers behind him. He abandoned his horse at Davenport Road, hid behind a log, and then "ran down through the College fields and avenue, keeping near the fence" (in present-day Queen's Park) until he reached Government House. For the third time that night, the weary lieutenant-governor was roused from his sleep. When he saw Powell, greatly distressed, and so out-of-breath from running through the streets that he could hardly tell his story, Head was convinced at last that an attack on Toronto was imminent.[14] Just as Powell was coming down the stairs, he met Colonel FitzGibbon ascending, on his third visit that night to Lieutenant-Governor Head. There was no argument this time. Head got dressed and FitzGibbon escorted him to City Hall.

There they found that Chief Justice Robinson, Attorney-General Hagerman, Judge Jonas Jones, and others who had scoffed at FitzGibbon's warnings had responded to the alarm and were taking up arms. On his own initiative Judge Jones organized a detachment of volunteers, which he led to the toll-gate just south of Bloor on Yonge Street, and remained there on guard for the rest of the night. Sentries posted elsewhere intercepted and imprisoned two horsemen riding to the city, probably messengers sent by Mackenzie to friends in Toronto. From them FitzGibbon heard of Colonel Moodie's death.

To the rebels assembled at Montgomery's Tavern,

the death of Captain Anderson came as a tragic shock. In the absence of Van Egmond, who had not yet arrived, they had counted on Anderson to lead the attack on Toronto. Now they could hear the city bells ringing in the frosty air and they realized that the people of Toronto were being alerted. They were disturbed by rumours that steamboats of loyalists were arriving in the city, and they were disappointed that Mackenzie had failed to bring any news.

After a sleepless night, Colonel FitzGibbon and four others, accompanied by Captain Frederick Halkett, aide-de-camp to Sir Francis Head, rode up Yonge Street until they came within sight of the rebel headquarters. They had heard that the rebels were placing barricades across the road, but they saw no sign of any obstruction. This was the time to attack, FitzGibbon thought. He had organized 500 volunteers into platoons and he proposed taking 300 of them and a six-pounder gun to march on Montgomery's. Head stubbornly refused permission. "I will not fight them on their ground", he said, "they must fight me on mine!" FitzGibbon felt exasperated. He was convinced that an immediate attack would bring prompt defeat to the rebels,[15] and he was surely right. The rebels were disheartened after the unfortunate events of the previous night; they were disorganized, lacked a competent military leader, and were poorly armed. Though more men had arrived during the night, bringing their number to 700 or 800, many of them were without arms. An attack that morning would have thrown them into confusion.

The rebels had to find a new military leader, and they chose Mackenzie, though he lacked military experience. Lount refused to act, and Van Egmond had still not arrived. (One may well ask if anyone was ever less fitted than Mackenzie to be a military commander. Untrained and excitable, he was better qualified to fight with tongue or pen than with a gun). The food problem at the camp had been solved, but the rebels remained wary of making that crucial attack on Toronto. It was nearly noon before "General" Mackenzie, mounted on a white pony, and protected against the cold (or was it against bullets?) by several layers of coats, led the insurgents on their deferred march to Toronto. They moved in one body until they reached Gallows Hill (just south of St Clair Avenue) where they divided into two columns, one under Mackenzie and the other under Lount. The final advance on the city was set for two p.m.

After his return to the city, Colonel FitzGibbon got busy organizing and arming volunteers, establishing posts at Government House, the Parliament Building, City Hall and the banks, while the lieutenant-governor attended to other matters. Head placed his family and that of Chief Justice Robinson in a steamer in the harbour, ready for flight if the city should be attacked. He had Mackenzie's house searched, but apparently Mackenzie's wife had burned most of the incriminating papers. When Sir Francis heard that "thousands" of rebels were converging on Montgomery's Tavern, he conceived the idea of offering a truce, perhaps to gain time until the militia volunteers would arrive from outlying parts of the province. Head wanted the flag of truce to be carried by someone the rebels would trust and, after prolonged negotiations, he persuaded the two Reformers, Robert Baldwin and Dr John Rolph, to deliver his message.

As the rebels waited at Gallows Hill for the hour when they were to begin their march on the city, they were surprised to see a party of three advancing from Toronto on horseback, bearing a large flag. They were even more surprised when they recognized the truce-bearers as Baldwin and Rolph, accompanied by a flag-bearer, a Toronto carpenter named Hugh Carmichael. Dr Rolph spoke for the lieutenant-governor, offering to grant an amnesty if the insurgents would disperse, and asking them to state their demands. Lount and Mackenzie conferred, after which Mackenzie announced their terms: "Independence and a convention to arrange the details", along with a request that the lieutenant-governor's reply be put in writing. The rebel leaders promised, on their part, that they would advance no farther than the Bloor Street toll-gate, while waiting for Head's response.[16]

When Baldwin and Rolph reported Mackenzie's terms to Head, he decided to withdraw the promise of amnesty, and sent the two men back with the message. Dr Rolph was in a very ambiguous position, known to the rebels as an ally, but now speaking for the lieutenant-governor. On one of his meetings with the insurgents (Rolph claimed it was the second occasion), he indicated that he was still on their side and he advised them to proceed with their planned attack that day.

At this point, Mackenzie had difficulty persuading his men to march. Mackenzie tried to encourage them by saying that the city was poorly defended, but he too showed unmistakable signs of nervousness. While the troops ate their meal, he and a few insurgents set fire to the house of Dr R.C. Horne, a Tory employed by the Bank of Upper Canada. Mackenzie tried to justify his action by saying that Horne's house was a rendezvous for spies. But many of his men were so disgusted with his uncalled-for act that they deserted and returned home. Later in the afternoon, Dr Rolph sent a messenger to Mackenzie inquiring about the cause of his delay and indicating that friends of the rebels were waiting in the city to join them when they arrived. On the strength of this message, Mackenzie assured his men that they would receive support when they entered the city. By six p.m. the rebels had assembled at the toll-gate, ready to march on Toronto.

Meanwhile, the officer who was responsible for preparing the militia to defend the city began acting in a nervous excitable way, much like Mackenzie. When one of the volunteers, Colonel William Chisholm of Oakville, insisted on taking a keg of ball cartridges that Colonel FitzGibbon had reserved for the attacking force, he spoke to Chisholm as if to a disobedient private: "Quit the wagon this instant, Sir, or I'll cut you down!" That evening, his composure restored, FitzGibbon prepared a guard of 27 men to be placed on Yonge Street, one kilometre south of the toll-gate. Lieutenant-Governor Head objected. "Do not send out a man!" he commanded. For the first time in his life, FitzGibbon disobeyed an order of the Queen's representative. "From what I had seen of night-fighting", he wrote afterwards, "I knew full well that a handful of men opening a fire upon them [the rebels] as they advanced, would at once make them run back. Whereas if they were not resisted they might come in with the more confidence and set fire to the city . . . . I therefore formed a piquet in a place where His Excellency could not see

Rebels marching down Yonge Street to attack Toronto in December 1837, by C.W. Jefferys

me, and placed Mr Sheriff [William Botsford] Jarvis at the head of it, and marched it out myself and posted it". The colonel then reported his action to Head who "rebuked me for it . . . but in milder terms than I expected from him".[17]

Shortly after six p.m., the rebels began marching south from the toll-gate in the dark December night: three abreast, the riflemen in the front ranks, followed by the pikemen, then by some dozens bearing old shotguns, and last of all by those who had only clubs and sticks. As soon as the absurd army of invaders drew opposite the sheriff's guard, which they could not see, Jarvis ordered his men to fire. They did, then promptly turned on their heels and fled, helter-skelter, back to the city. On Lount's command to the rebels to return the fire, the front rank fired their rifles, then threw themselves on the ground to let those behind shoot over them. In the darkness, the rear ranks, noticing that the men in front had fallen, thought they had been killed or wounded and, like the sheriff's men, they took to their heels in flight. Mackenzie could not get them to stop running until they reached the toll-gate.

The comic-opera battle was over. The rebels refused to make another advance that night. They would go by daylight, they told Mackenzie, but not in the dark. Just as Colonel FitzGibbon had foreseen, a few shots in the dark by a very small force produced panic among the advancing insurgents. He had not foreseen that his own men would likewise be overcome with panic. Nevertheless, the guard had achieved its purpose.

Later that night, Head summoned FitzGibbon and ordered him to have the arms moved from City Hall to the Parliament Building. He had received an anonymous letter telling him that the rebels intended to set fire to the city and he thought that the position of the City Hall in close proximity to other buildings made it too difficult to protect, whereas the Parliament Building had open space around it. The colonel acknowledged the logic of Head's argument but he thought it unwise to try to move the munitions at that hour of the night. He feared that if the volunteers were taken from their posts to transport the arms and boxes of ammunition on foot (no wagons were available), great confusion would ensue, and besides, the volunteers might take advantage of the opportunity to go home for rest and refreshment. While FitzGibbon was trying to think of a way out of this dilemma without further antagonizing the lieutenant-governor, Colonel Allan MacNab arrived from Hamilton with 60 militiamen from the District of Gore. "Now, Sir, we are safe till morning, for with this reinforcement we can guard every approach", said FitzGibbon, and Head accepted the argument, though in fact, the 60 militiamen added little to the security of the city. The next day FitzGibbon had the arms and ammunition moved by wagons and carts from City Hall to the Parliament Building, where he posted additional guards.

Throughout Wednesday, 6 December, volunteers poured in to Toronto from the country. They marched from the eastern counties and from the Lake Simcoe area in the north, and boatloads of militiamen came from the districts of Niagara and Gore. By sunset that day, some 1,200 volunteers had arrived, and more came the next day. The lieutenant-governor estimated, with some exaggeration, that about 10,000 men flocked to Toronto to offer their services. The unusual number of men roaming about the small city, waiting to be organized for action, created a problem for the acting adjutant-general. He considered it imperative to make the attack on the rebels on Thursday. He kept expecting Lieutenant-Governor Head to order the attack, but the day passed and no order came.

In desperation on Wednesday evening, Colonel FitzGibbon resolved to seek out Head and broach the question of attacking the rebels the next day. He learned that the lieutenant-governor was at Archdeacon Strachan's elegant Georgian "palace" on Front Street. Before going there, FitzGibbon took the precaution of asking Solicitor-General William Henry Draper and Executive Councillor William Allan to accompany him and lend their support to his argument. They found Attorney-General Hagerman and the Honourable R.B. Sullivan with Head and Strachan. In the prolonged discussion that followed, FitzGibbon sensed a curious reluctance to agree to the attack, but finally the lieutenant-governor gave his consent. FitzGibbon then rose to leave, but the Honourable William Allan drew him back. This forthright man, who had risen to his influential position by sheer ability, without the usual educational and family advantages of Family Compact members, and who had interceded on FitzGibbon's behalf the preceding Saturday, now spoke up again. "I apprehend there is some misunderstanding here", he said. "It is plain from what Colonel FitzGibbon has said this evening, that he expects to command at the attack! . . . But Colonel Macnab told me this day, that His Excellency promised him the command!" After an embarrassing pause, Hagerman commented, "Why, as His Excellency has appointed Colonel Macnab to command the Militia in the Home District, it is a matter in course that he should command at the attack". It was news to the acting adjutant-general that MacNab had been appointed head of the Home District militia, and he sat in shocked silence while this exchange took place.

FitzGibbon had assumed all along that he would lead the attack. He protested to Hagerman that it wasn't at all a matter of course that the Home District militia commander should lead the force assembled to march against the rebels. Then he learned that Colonel MacNab had proposed attacking the rebels at three in the morning, an hour when, in FitzGibbon's opinion, the attempt would be bound to fail. It would be utterly impossible, he thought, "to organize the confused Mass of human beings then congregated in the City during the night-time". FitzGibbon felt especially upset and even insulted by the selection of MacNab as commander instead of himself, for, he reasoned, "I was a Colonel of Militia before Mr MacNab had any rank in that Force, and he was almost wholly without military knowledge".[18] Allan MacNab had been a boy of 14 when the War of 1812 broke out, but he saw action nevertheless and in 1814 was promoted to ensign in the 49th Regiment. He became lieutenant-colonel of the Gore 4th Militia Regiment in 1830 and colonel six years later, but this experience had involved no military action. Sir Francis Bond Head, however, greatly admired this assertive and imposing man. Long after the rebellion was over, Head wrote that when MacNab arrived with his boatload of "the men of Gore", his own "most ardent hopes [were] suddenly realized", for, he said, "of all the individuals in the province whom I could most have desired to see combined with me in arms to defend it, was the very one who first came to the British standard – namely, the Speaker of the Commons' House of Assembly".[19]

When FitzGibbon withdrew from the meeting at the Archdeacon's residence, no final decision had been made as to who would command. The colonel felt very uneasy, as he made the round of his posts before retiring to his office in the Parliament House at one a.m.

In the insurgents' camp, Wednesday had passed gloomily. There were only about 600 men left at Montgomery's but more were expected from the west, and Colonel Van Egmond would arrive the next day. The three leaders — Mackenzie, Lount and Gibson — decided to wait for Van Egmond's arrival and attack the city on Thursday, as they had planned originally. Mackenzie, however, perhaps feeling unbearably restless, rode with some of his men to the Peacock Inn on Dundas Street, where they held up the west-bound mail stage, seized the mail-bags and took captive the driver and some passengers. The reason Mackenzie gave afterwards for this action was that he had thereby succeeded in intercepting letters from government officials containing the information that they expected soon to attack the rebels. He denied the charge that he had taken money from the mail.

While this piece of brigandage was being enacted in the cause of rebellion, a radical doctor and rebel sympathizer, T.D. Morrison, was arrested in Toronto while making his house calls. The arrest was observed by one of Dr Rolph's medical students, who hastened to report it to his superior. Within a few minutes, the student mounted the doctor's gray colt, rode it to the western outskirts of the city where he waited until Dr Rolph arrived on foot, calm and unhurried. Rolph rode off towards Queenston and the following morning he crossed the Niagara River to the United States.

On Thursday morning, Colonel FitzGibbon wakened at four and began drafting a plan of attack. But he was oppressed by the uncertainty of his position and the seriousness of the situation. When two prominent government officials, Judge James Macaulay and Surveyor-General John Macaulay, dropped by his office, he asked them to call on the lieutenant-governor in his temporary quarters at the other end of the Parliament House and inquire concerning his decision on the proposed attack. Soon after, FitzGibbon and MacNab were summoned to Head's presence. The sun had not yet risen, and they found Sir Francis in a camp bed, still in his night-clothes. He was in a ridiculous situation for a conference, but the pompous little lieutenant-governor drew himself up in bed and delivered a short speech. He was in a painful position, he said, being confronted by "two officers of equal zeal, of equal bravery, and of equal talent competing for the command". These words were very offensive to FitzGibbon. As an officer noted for partisan activity and an heroic coup in the War of 1812, he rightly felt that his military experience greatly surpassed that of MacNab. He protested vehemently, whereupon Head asked him and the Macaulays to withdraw. They waited in the cold unheated corridor for half an hour, while Head conferred with MacNab. When they were called back, Head said that Colonel MacNab had released him from his promise and that Colonel FitzGibbon was to have the command. FitzGibbon shook hands with his 39-year-old rival, against whom he bore no personal grudge, and hastened to carry out his assignment.

Now the accumulated tension of the last few days, combined with fatigue due to lack of sleep, almost caused Colonel FitzGibbon to lose his self-control just when he most needed good judgment and the ability to act effectively. "It was now broad daylight and I had to commence an organization of the most difficult nature I had ever known", FitzGibbon recorded afterwards. In fact, apart from arranging the ambush at Beaver Dams, he had never before been called upon to organize troops for battle. He embarked on a round of feverish activity.

> I had to ride to the Town Hall, to the Garrison and back again, repeatedly. I found few of the officers present who were wanted for the attack. Vast numbers

> of Volunteers were constantly coming in from the Country without arms or appointments of any kind, who were crowding in all directions in my way. My mind was burning with indignation at the idea of Col. MacNab or any other Militia Officer being thought of by His Excellency for the Command, after all I had hitherto done for him. My difficulties multiplied upon me; time, of all things the most precious, was wasting for want of ammunition, for want of Officers, for the want of most of my men from the Town Hall, whose Commander was yet absent, till at length the organization appeared impossible. I became overwhelmed with the intensity and contrariety of my feelings, I walked to and fro without object until I observed the eyes of many fixed upon me, when I fled to my room and locked my door, exclaiming audibly, that the Province was lost, that I was ruined, fallen. For let it not be forgotten, that it was admitted at the conference at the Archdeacon's the evening before that if the attack of the next day should fail that the Province would be lost. This however, then was not my opinion, but I thought of my present failure after the efforts I had made to obtain the command and the evil consequences likely to flow from that failure and I did then despair.

FitzGibbon fell on his knees and prayed for strength, and strength came to him. When he emerged from his office he found that one company had been formed. He marched it to the road in front of Archdeacon Strachan's palace, "and having once begun I sent company after company, and gun after gun until the whole stood in order".[20]

By noon, the force was ready. It was drawn up in three columns. Colonel MacNab was in command of the main or centre column of some 700 men; Colonel Samuel Peters Jarvis had the right wing (200), and Colonel Archibald McLean the left (not quite 200 men). MacNab's column was to march up Yonge Street while the right wing would move north by an easterly route and the left would go by a road west of Yonge. The three columns were to converge at Montgomery's Tavern.

It was one of those clear frosty days without a cloud in the sky. Even the lieutenant-governor was infected by the thrill of the occasion. He recollected afterwards that, "I was sitting on horseback waiting to hear the officer commanding the assembled force order his men to advance, and was wondering why he did not do so, when one of the principal leaders rode up to me, and told me that the militia wished me to give them the word of command, which I accordingly did". Colonel FitzGibbon was very jealous of his right to command, and made it clear in his account of the day's events that "This was the only command he [Head] gave till the action was over. I led the Column to the attack, directed every movement personally".

The troops marched up Yonge Street to the music of two bands, while women and children and men too old to fight stood at windows and on housetops, waving flags and cheering the brave volunteers on their way. Colonel FitzGibbon rode proudly in the vanguard, pleased that his two sons, William aged 18 and James only 16, were by his side. (Charles was still in Ireland).

In the meantime, Colonel Van Egmond had arrived at Montgomery's Tavern early Thursday morning to find that the assembled company was reduced to around 500. There was some hope that reinforcements would arrive later that day, but as it turned out, no more men came. The rebel leaders disagreed on the best plan to follow and wasted precious time in argument. At last they decided to create a diversion east of Toronto in the hope of drawing off the government troops in that direction. About ten a.m. Peter Mathews, a radical farmer, led a party of 60 to the Don bridge. The party was to set fire to the bridge and the nearby tavern and also to intercept the Montreal mail. The rest of the insurgents would march towards the city or do whatever else might be required. Matthews' detachment succeeded in intercepting the mail and in burning the tavern and stable, but as the men saw the eastern column of loyalist troops approaching, they realized that they were greatly outnumbered and they retreated. The diversionary measure was a failure.

About one p.m., the sentinels at Montgomery's reported seeing the government troops advancing. Mackenzie and Van Egmond hastily deployed their men, some in the woods to the west of the tavern, others beyond the fence to the east. Those who were unarmed remained inside. Soon two cannon balls crashed through the walls of the tavern and there was a sudden outpouring of men from the inn, "exuding from the door like bees from the little hole of their hive", as Sir Francis picturesquely described it. David Gibson emerged from the back door and set the prisoners free. The fighting between the government troops and the rebels in the woods lasted no more than 20 minutes. The rebels were easily put to rout.

The loyalists showed little better discipline than the rebels. A man on horseback was seen riding up to the door of the tavern with the apparent intention of riding right through the doorway. Colonel MacNab called out, "Shoot me that man!" Two volunteers advanced, took aim, and were about to fire when someone shouted, "Don't fire! It's Judge Jones!"[21] Thus did the "over zeal" of the judge in the excitement of battle nearly cost him his life. FitzGibbon with a small party of men set off in pursuit of Mackenzie who had been seen riding off in flight. One of the men saw Mackenzie abandon his horse and disappear into the forest. The pursuers gave up the chase. A reward of £1,000 was offered by the government that day for the capture of Mackenzie, and £500 for David Gibson, Samuel Lount, Jesse Lloyd or Silas Fletcher.

As FitzGibbon's party turned south to rejoin the main column, they saw black clouds of smoke rising from the tavern. The lieutenant-governor had ordered that it be set on fire in revenge against John Montgomery for providing a rendezvous for the insurgents, and to avenge Colonel Moodie's death. Soon FitzGibbon met a detachment of militia coming towards him, on their way to burn Gibson's house, as ordered by Sir Francis. But now his aide-de-camp, Henry Sherwood, arrived to rescind the order. Then Head changed his mind again. He sent for FitzGibbon and said, "Let Gibson's house be burned immediately, and let the Militia be kept here until it is done". When the colonel started to protest, Head became angry and repeated the order. It was then near sunset and the December evening was turning cold. The men were tired and hungry. One of the officers refused to set fire to the house, so FitzGibbon carried out the order himself with the aid of a small detachment. Mrs Gibson and her four small children had to seek refuge at a neighbouring farm.

When FitzGibbon arrived home about seven p.m., he was "reduced to the last degree of exhaustion by fatigue, cold and want of food and rest". He had to be helped off his horse and supported into the house. But greater than his bodily fatigue, and almost obliterating his satisfaction over leading the militia to victory, was his resentment towards Lieutenant-Governor Head for having tried to deprive him of the command.[22]

Chapter Eight

Disillusioned, Humiliated and Embittered

Mackenzie had fled, the back of the rebellion was broken, and Colonel James FitzGibbon, more than any other single individual, deserved the credit for the victory. But perversely, in what should have been his days of exultation, FitzGibbon's strongest emotion was one of hurt pride over the way Sir Francis Bond Head had treated him. He was exhausted by the tension and events of the preceding fortnight: his efforts to arouse the government to the danger of insurrection, the uncertainty about who would lead the attack, the excitement of the attack itself and the burning of Gibson's house.

On the morning after the battle, Chief Justice Robinson called on FitzGibbon to inquire of his health. Robinson, like Jones, Hagerman and Head, had deplored FitzGibbon's warnings, but now he magnanimously gave the colonel credit for his vigilance in preventing a surprise attack by the rebels. FitzGibbon was confined to his bed and his thoughts were morose. "My mind became exasperated at the wrongs which had been intended for me, after my having made efforts almost superhuman in defence of the City and the Province. . . . I resolved to retire from the Militia Staff of His Excellency, from a conviction that no cordiality or good will could exist between us".[1] He asked the chief justice to convey orally to the lieutenant-governor his resignation as acting adjutant-general of militia. This was an impetuous and ill-tempered gesture that FitzGibbon had cause later to regret.

It was rumoured in Toronto that the colonel's mind had been affected by the strain of the crisis. Colonel C.L.L. Foster, commander of the military forces in Upper Canada, wrote in a confidential letter to Sir John Colborne that, "The excitement created . . . by such an attempted act of injustice from the Lt. Governor to FitzGibbon actually drove him *mad*" – an exaggerated statement, but it probably reflected the talk of the town. In his own "Narrative of Occurrences" describing the events of the rebellion, FitzGibbon admitted that the lieutenant-governor's hostility "nearly destroyed the tone of my mind. I have, however, survived it and will still continue my efforts in the public service".[2] This narrative was dated 13 December 1837, less than a week after the battle with the rebels, so it would appear that his derangement was of short duration.

Within that week, however, FitzGibbon made a foolish request. Ignoring the ill-will that existed between himself and Sir Francis Head, he asked that he be permitted to take the official despatches on the rebellion to England. FitzGibbon's object was a personal one. He wanted to be sent abroad so he could go to Ireland to see his son Charles and his brothers, whom he had not seen since 1802. Perhaps he hoped also to make some arrangement about his debts. After some consideration of the request, Head declined. FitzGibbon felt rebuffed and more resentful than ever. He responded to the lieutenant-governor with a querulous letter in which he showed his resentment towards Head and laid the blame for the non-payment of his debts on those who had refused to promote him.

> I will here declare that I would have served Your Excellency most faithfully, but the die is cast, Your Excellency has declined to comply with an earnest request of mine, after all I have done for Your Excellency and the Province, and the future promises me little even to hope for . . . .
>
> For forty years I have served my Country and

> have ever been in debt and distress since I obtained my first Commission in 1806, because of the extraordinary efforts I have made, and the inferior and unproductive offices to which I have, hitherto, been confined. I desire neither rank, honor, nor applause – I desire simply to be enabled to pay my debts and to live in humble independence with my Family; for my pecuniary embarrassments are becoming quite intolerable to me.[3]

A few days later, James wrote to his brother Henry in Dublin, telling him about his disappointment in not being sent "home" with the despatches, and describing proudly the part he had played in "preserving this city from destruction, and the province . . . from unknown calamities". He emphasized that "I conducted the whole myself", and he went on to state that "the young men of my old rifle company were the real fighting men of the day". James wrote of his exhaustion. "I have not left my room since the evening of the 7th. The efforts I made, mental and bodily, were beyond my strength . . . and the nature of the sinister attempt to deprive me of the command, operated most injuriously upon me". This letter had an unfortunate result. It was intended for family eyes only, but Henry FitzGibbon sent it to the *Dublin Evening Mail*, which published it on 24 January 1838. The *Gazette* of Hamilton, Upper Canada, reprinted the letter along with editorial comment accusing FitzGibbon of egotism and vanity and of overlooking the contribution of the militia in the province's defence. FitzGibbon was further embarrassed when the Toronto *Patriot* of 27 April commented on the affair and reprinted the letter of explanation that he had sent to the *Hamilton Gazette*.

Meanwhile the militia under Colonel Allan MacNab had suppressed the uprising led by Charles Duncombe in the western part of the province in December, and in January, with naval support, had driven Mackenzie from Navy Island in the Niagara River. FitzGibbon raised no objections to MacNab's appointment as leader of these expeditions, since he was no longer acting as adjutant-general.

Even before the rebellion had finally run its course on Navy Island, Lieutenant-Governor Head began trying to counteract the accusation that he had been tardy in taking steps to put down the insurrection. In a despatch to Colonial Secretary Lord Glenelg, dated 19 December 1837, Head stated that he had been in command of the situation throughout, and that he had been aware of Mackenzie's activities but had considered it wiser to await the outbreak. Head made no mention of Colonel FitzGibbon's repeated warnings nor of the latter's preparations to counter an attack. He implied that the picket on Yonge Street, commanded by Sheriff Jarvis, had been his idea. His first and only reference to FitzGibbon was in connection with the march up Yonge Street: "Accordingly, on Thursday morning I assembled our forces under the direction of the adjutant-general of militia, Colonel Fitzgibbon, [*sic*], clerk of the House of Assembly". Head then gave a glowing account of the battle. He mentioned the burning of Montgomery's Tavern and the Gibson house but omitted saying that he had ordered the fires to be set. He gave credit to the militia, while justifying his own action: "I . . . called upon the militia of Upper Canada to defend me, and the result has been . . . that the people of Upper Canada came to me when I called them; that they completely defeated Mr M'Kenzie's [*sic*] adherents, and drove him and his rebel ringleaders from the land".[4]

Parts of this despatch were published in the Toronto *Patriot* on 17 April 1838. It disturbed and angered Colonel FitzGibbon, who immediately drafted a letter to Lord Glenelg, drawing attention to the misleading statements made by Head. Glenelg never saw this letter because the new lieutenant-governor, Sir George Arthur, advised FitzGibbon to withdraw it. Wisely, FitzGibbon took his advice. At the time, measures were being taken in Upper Canada to reward him for his services.

Early in 1838, the Legislature of Upper Canada addressed a request to Queen Victoria praying that Her Majesty would be pleased to grant James FitzGibbon "five thousand acres of the waste lands of the Crown", and stating that he had

> rendered so great services to this Province, in a military capacity, on various occasions, when he was an Officer of the Regular Forces of the Empire, during the late

Parliament Buildings, Front Street, Toronto, as in 1832-1893

war with the United States of America, and subsequently in several civil capacities; and also very recently, as Colonel of Militia, in the breaking out of the late rebellion in the Home District.[5]

Sir George Arthur had not yet arrived when the Legislature took this step, so it fell to Sir Francis Head to forward the address. In doing so, Head sent a covering letter to Glenelg in which, surprisingly, he paid tribute to FitzGibbon as a loyal servant who had performed well both in war and in peace. Head sent FitzGibbon a copy of this letter and, in a further effort at conciliation, invited the colonel to dine with him on the eve of his departure for England. On this occasion Head gave assurances that he would exert his best efforts with the British government on FitzGibbon's behalf.

In retrospect, Head's belated attempt to show appreciation of FitzGibbon's services appeared hypocritical. Soon after he left the province, Head's letter to Glenelg was published in the *Patriot*. It also became known that a month previous to forwarding the address to the Queen in the interest of FitzGibbon, Head had written to Glenelg, on his own initiative, asking that Allan MacNab be honoured with a knighthood for his part in putting down the rebellion and driving Mackenzie from Navy Island. Head asked that Chief Justice Robinson be knighted too, but Robinson declined the honour. MacNab was duly created a knight bachelor later in 1838.

FitzGibbon was, of course, greatly pleased by Parliament's move to reward him. He regarded it as "the spontaneous proceedings of a whole people in my favour – a people among whom I lived and served for more than thirty years".[6] While waiting for the Queen's approval of the land grant, he was further delighted by a magnificent gesture on the part of the citizens of Toronto. At a testimonial meeting called by Mayor John Powell for 12 May, the Torontonians moved resolutions of appreciation to FitzGibbon for "rescuing them from the horrors of civil war", and stating

that upon the breaking out of the late Insurrection, the City of Toronto was, under Providence, saved from falling into the hands of the rebels by the active exertions

> of Colonel James Fitzgibbon, [*sic*], and others acting with him, on the night of Monday the 4th of December last.
>
> That Colonel FitzGibbon, during the 4th, 5th, 6th and 7th days of December last, and until the rebels dispersed, was actively and unremittingly employed, by night and by day, in organizing the inhabitants and volunteers who hastened to the post of danger, to defend the lives and property of the Citizens and to sustain the Constitution and Laws of the Country under which it is our happiness to live.[7]

The meeting resolved further that it regretted the way in which Sir Francis Bond Head had overlooked FitzGibbon's services in his letter to Lord Glenelg.

It was decided that subscription lists should be opened at the various banks for the purpose of receiving donations for a suitable memorial expressive of the city's gratitude to Colonel FitzGibbon. A committee was appointed to carry out the intentions of the meeting.

About two weeks later, the committee wrote to Lieutenant-Governor Arthur stating that it hoped a sum of money would be subscribed "sufficient to build a handsome cottage" for James FitzGibbon, and it asked for a grant of land on the former military reserve on which the cottage could be erected. The committee added that "it is intended to vest the property in the hands of Trustees in perpetuity, for the benefit of Colonel FitzGibbon and his heirs as a lasting memorial of the services of that gentleman to this City". This letter was signed by Mayor John Powell and his 12 committee members.[8]

Colonel FitzGibbon was elated. For the second time in his life he enjoyed a hero's acclaim. He rejoiced in the warmth of the tributes, and anticipated with pleasure the promised rewards and monetary value they represented. At last, he thought, he would be able to free himself of his heavy burden of debt. But FitzGibbon's elation was fated to evaporate like soap bubbles, leaving him a disillusioned and cynical man. The Toronto plan never materialized, and FitzGibbon had to wait years for the parliamentary reward. The city's request for land on which to build the cottage was brought before the provincial government. There it was stalled. It was argued in the

Legislature that the request from the city for an acre of land might adversely affect the provincial request for its grant of 5,000 acres. Both requests would have to be forwarded to the British government. The acre of land was never granted, and the citizens of Toronto took no further steps to reward Colonel FitzGibbon. Why this was so has not been made clear. Did the subscription campaign fail? Did opposition to the reward develop among some of the citizens for financial or other reasons? The *Patriot* was silent on the subject.

The disappointment rankled FitzGibbon. He attributed the refusal of the provincial government to act on the city's request to efforts made by some high government official to stop the proceedings. It was this official, according to FitzGibbon, who claimed that the city's request for one acre might counteract the effect of the provincial request to the British government. FitzGibbon did not name the official whom he blamed, but it seems likely that the man he had in mind was Christopher Hagerman, the attorney-general. It will be recalled that, prior to the outbreak of the rebellion, Hagerman had poured scorn on FitzGibbon's warnings and that he had shown a preference for MacNab to lead the attack on the rebels. To add to the bad feeling, FitzGibbon offended Hagerman on the march to Montgomery's Tavern. The colonel described the incident as follows:

> as we approached the position occupied by the Rebels, and on the point of commencing the attack, Mr Hagerman rode up to me and began to speak; when I said to him, "Do not speak to me, Mr Hagerman; I cannot hear you now". In an imperative tone he said, "You must hear me, Sir!" "Must hear you, Sir?" I replied, "Not a word from you, Sir, at your peril not another word from you!" and immediately I gave an order for the two guns to take a position and open upon the Rebels.[9]

FitzGibbon's exceptional rudeness was undoubtedly due to his intense nervousness at the time, combined with his resentment of Hagerman's previous treatment of him. Hagerman's feelings were not reported, but it may be taken for granted that he felt insulted and angry at the insolence of a man who, in civilian life, held a position far beneath his. Even in military experience, Hagerman had just cause for pride, for he had served with distinction in the War of 1812 and had become aide-de-camp to Lieutenant-General Gordon Drummond, with the militia rank of lieutenant-colonel.

Further disappointment was in store for FitzGibbon. Towards the end of June, word was received from Lord Glenelg that Her Majesty had refused consent to the provincial land grant because it would be inconsistent with the act of Upper Canada that dealt with the disposal of Crown lands. Her Majesty would be pleased, however, to give assent to a pecuniary grant for FitzGibbon if the two Houses of the Legislature were to pass such a measure. The 1837 land act of Upper Canada, to which reference was made, limited free grants of land to United Empire Loyalists and their children, and to other persons who were entitled to a grant by virtue of any government order-in-council or regulation in existence at the time the law was passed. The proposed grant to FitzGibbon did not qualify. Nothing further could be done about the reward until the opening of the 1839 session of Parliament.

Meanwhile, FitzGibbon's debts continued to grow. In expectation of the land grant he said he had taken on new responsibilities. He was probably referring to the care of his niece Margaret FitzGibbon, who came from Ireland to Toronto after the death of her father, James' brother Thomas. (She accompanied her cousin Charles FitzGibbon when he returned from Dublin to practise law in Toronto). From that time on, Margaret lived as a member of her uncle's family.

James FitzGibbon was now in serious financial straits. His debt of £2,000, mentioned in his memorial to Head, had increased by at least £1,500, which he had borrowed from an old friend Major Brock of Colchester, England. (Major Brock was the father of George Brock who accompanied the colonel on the ride up Yonge Street on the night of 4 December 1837). Even if FitzGibbon had received the 5,000 acres of land in 1838 and sold it at the current value of two shillings an acre, he would still have been heavily in debt. Of course, in the early stages of his delight over the promised reward, he had visions of selling the land for ten shillings per acre.

Surprisingly, in view of his preoccupation with his debts and his promised reward, James FitzGibbon took time in the summer of 1838 to prepare a paper, "Observations on the Canadas", for Lord Durham, who had arrived in Quebec in May 1838 as governor-in-chief of British North America, with instructions to examine the causes of the two provincial rebellions and to make recommendations for the future. In his paper, FitzGibbon stated that he was opposed to union with Lower Canada. By uniting the two provinces, he said, "you turn from Great Britain the hearts of many devoted Loyalists who are more averse to connexion with Lower Canada than they are to connexion with the United States". This statement reflected the viewpoint on provincial union that was held by many Upper Canadian conservatives of the time. The greater part of FitzGibbon's "Observations", however, dealt with the problem of defence against possible invasion or absorption by the United States.[10] It is not known how Lord Durham reacted to this paper.

Later that summer FitzGibbon's hostility towards Sir Francis Bond Head was roused again by an "Explanatory Memorandum" which the former lieutenant-governor addressed to Lord Glenelg and which was published in the Toronto *Patriot* of 3 August. As before, Head argued that his apparent lack of response to the threatened insurrection had been a cleverly calculated policy. He stated, moreover, that he had consulted with Colonel FitzGibbon almost daily about the plan to be followed should the rebels attack the city. When the crisis came, Head said, he summoned the militia, and "10,000 men, in the depth of winter, at once rushed to my assistance". FitzGibbon quickly responded to the memorandum by presenting his version of the events in a long letter to Lord Glenelg. In particular he reported the facts about the burning of Gibson's house and about the sheriff's guard on Yonge Street, saying that the lieutenant-governor "positively forbade me to send a man out"; that he had defied the order and shortly afterwards "this very Picquet repulsed the Rebels . . . and saved the Town". FitzGibbon declared that in the period preceding the revolt, Sir Francis had resisted every suggestion that was made for defence, and had his course been followed, the province would have fallen to the rebels.[11]

Realizing that he could no longer hope for early relief from his desperate financial situation, FitzGibbon directed his efforts to obtaining a better position. It became known in September 1838 that George Markland had resigned his post as inspector-general of public provincial accounts. A mystery surrounded Markland's resignation. He was accused of immoral conduct. Lieutenant-Governor Arthur ordered an investigation by the Executive Council, in the midst of which Markland resigned and thereafter faded from public life. (It is now known that Markland was accused of homosexuality). FitzGibbon decided to try once again for the position of inspector-general, though he was no better qualified for the post than before. He wrote a letter of application to John Macaulay, who had become the lieutenant-governor's civil secretary. Ironically, and of course unknown to FitzGibbon, Macaulay was the lieutenant-governor's choice for the vacant position. It happened, however, that another high-ranking office became available just then, due to the death of Duncan Cameron, provincial secretary and registrar for the previous 20 years. The yearly salary for this position was £600 as compared with £565 for that of inspector-general. FitzGibbon wrote again to Macaulay asking to be appointed to either of the two offices, and emphasizing his need for relief from his financial problems. He received neither appointment. Sir George Arthur was intent upon reorganizing some government departments, and James FitzGibbon formed no part of his plans.

Like Sir Peregrine Maitland and Sir John Colborne, Major-General Sir George Arthur had a military background, but no sympathetic bond developed between him and James FitzGibbon as had happened with Maitland and Colborne. Before his appointment in Upper Canada, Arthur had served as lieutenant-governor and military commander of British Honduras (where he quelled a Negro slave insurrection), and afterwards of Van Diemen's Land (Tasmania), the British penal colony. In those two places, he acquired a reputation of ruling with courage and firmness. As to character, Arthur was considered stern, upright and practical. When the two Upper Canadian rebels Samuel Lount and Peter Mathews were sentenced to be hanged for treason, Sir George Arthur refused to pardon them, though pleas for pardon came from all parts of the province, and one petition for Lount contained 5,000 names.

Arthur's approach to the government of Upper Canada was one of efficiency. He took the first step towards reorganization in June 1838 when he persuaded John Macaulay to give up his post of surveyor-general to become civil secretary in the lieutenant-governor's office. This move enabled Arthur to amalgamate the positions of surveyor-general and commissioner of crown lands. When the position of inspector-general of public accounts became available, Arthur kept the promise he had made to Macaulay to appoint him to the first office comparable in salary and prestige to that of surveyor-general that might become vacant.

Duncan Cameron's death opened the way for change in the office of provincial secretary, which Sir George Arthur proposed enlarging to include some of the functions of his own civil secretary. His nominee for the post was Richard Alexander Tucker, a Bermuda-born colonial officer who had formerly been chief justice of Newfoundland but who had resigned that position over a difference with the Newfoundland Legislature. Lord Glenelg had drawn Tucker to the attention of Lieutenant-Governor Arthur, so that his subsequent nomination as provincial secretary and registrar was rapidly approved. Afterwards Arthur appointed Tucker to the Executive Council.

FitzGibbon was upset by the choice of Tucker as provincial secretary, and he addressed a letter of protest to the colonial secretary. Sir George Arthur forwarded the letter to Lord Glenelg, along with one from another rejected applicant, Samuel Peters Jarvis (formerly Cameron's deputy), who also wished to have his case reviewed. In his accompanying letter to Lord Glenelg, Sir George Arthur commented fairly and objectively on James FitzGibbon, describing him as "a very old public servant and a worthy and highly honorable person", who was suffering from pecuniary embarrassment and was hoping for an office that would provide him with a larger income to which he felt entitled as a reward for his services to the province.

Arthur's detached analysis of FitzGibbon's plight was in sharp contrast to the tone of FitzGibbon's own account of his situation in his letter to Lord Glenelg. FitzGibbon began with a reference to his 40-year service to his country, then went on to say that he had been "wronged and injured by Sir Francis Head who of all men was most indebted to me"; that, although he had saved the city and hence the province from the rebels, he was left to struggle "in the greatest extremity of pecuniary embarrassment"; and that he had been denied offices that would have saved him from ruin. Even the promised grant of land from the province had been refused, he complained, and he was convinced that the proposed alternative of a pecuniary grant would not be acted upon by the House of Assembly. In short, he was confronted wherever he turned "by the most discouraging treatment" and therefore, "I pray of your Lordship to set aside the appointment of the person placed in the office of Secretary and Register and to order that I be appointed thereto".

FitzGibbon assured Lord Glenelg that he did not wish to be offensive and, obviously conscious that his letter would be read by Sir George Arthur, he stated in conclusion that he held for His Excellency "sentiments of the highest respect . . . unmixed with any adverse feeling which may be supposed to influence my present proceedings".[12]

The only apparent result of FitzGibbon's letter was the offer, made the following year by Lieutenant-Governor Arthur, of a shrievalty in the District of Niagara. FitzGibbon refused the post, saying that "I have had an insurmountable repugnance to witness the sufferings and misery of human beings immersed in Prisons, or having their property seized for debt". Consequently, he continued in his letter to Arthur, he had resolved never to accept such an office.[13] FitzGibbon may also have feared the insecurity of being sheriff. No salary was attached to the position, but fees in the Niagara District could go as high as £765 a year.

At this stage in his career, FitzGibbon must surely have regretted his hasty resignation as acting adjutant-general of militia. Nathaniel Coffin had finally retired as adjutant-general in late 1837 and had been replaced by Captain Richard Bullock, just 11 days after FitzGibbon, in wounded pride, had resigned. The position of adjutant-general was one for which FitzGibbon was ideally suited with his army background and his previous experience in the militia office. However, he had told Sir Francis Head, prior to the rebellion, that he would never accept the office. He had made this impulsive declaration when Head had consulted him on the state of the adjutant-general's department, and the colonel had given a very unfavourable report. Head then asked FitzGibbon why he had not imparted this information before, to which the latter replied, "Had I done so Your Excellency might have supposed that I desired to have the Adjutant General dismissed and myself appointed in his stead, but now that I have made this statement to Your Excellency, I never will accept the Office".[14] Nevertheless, as we have seen, during the crisis of December 1837, FitzGibbon did agree to act in that post and it is quite possible that, if he had not taken offence at Sir Francis Head subsequently, he might have been willing to accept the permanent appointment.

It was Sir George Arthur's view that, in resigning as acting adjutant-general of militia, FitzGibbon "had acted unwisely".[15] FitzGibbon's lack of advancement in the future substantiated this opinion. While in the past the post of adjutant-general of militia had not been as rewarding as that of Assembly clerk (taking into account the £180 for extra services that the latter received annually in addition to his salary), an adjustment was made to the salary in December 1837 and within two years it was established at £540 (sterling). When FitzGibbon resigned as acting adjutant-general, he rashly cast aside his best chance of promotion to one of the higher-paying positions in the province.

James FitzGibbon was approaching the age of 60. He had lost much of his vigour and geniality. He was becoming increasingly obsessed with the pressure of his debts and consequently with his urgent desire to obtain his reward. As he had foreseen, the House of Assembly, in its 1839 session, avoided granting FitzGibbon a pecuniary award. The members thought that the province could not afford this expenditure in its debt-ridden circumstances. Instead, the House introduced a new bill granting him the 5,000 acres previously suggested, taking care to word the bill in such a way as to circumvent (the Assembly hoped) the terms of the Public Lands Act. But Sir George Arthur considered that the bill amounted to a repeal of that Act, and he reserved it for the Queen's approval. When the scrupulous lieutenant-governor refused to sanction the 1839 version of the bill, FitzGibbon became agitated and rushed off to England.

Impulsively, FitzGibbon decided to plead his own case with the British authorities. He left Canada in such a hurry that he had no time to obtain leave of absence nor to pay the accounts that were charged to his office. Furthermore, he was so angry at Sir George Arthur for reserving the bill (which FitzGibbon considered unnecessary), that he addressed an offensive letter to the lieutenant-governor before he set sail from Montreal. In this letter, which ran to several pages, FitzGibbon said that in reserving the land-grant bill the lieutenant-governor had caused a delay during which some of the most valuable Crown land would be taken up. He charged that Sir George Arthur looked down upon him, and that he had commented from time to time that he (FitzGibbon) "was entitled to but little credit for the capture of an American Detachment during the late War". He referred to the crisis in his affairs: "By injustice am I driven almost to despair, and to desperation, having only one hope left in an appeal to Her Majesty's Government in England". He complained that although he had saved Toronto and the province in 1837, "Sir Francis Head and Your Excellency have each given Offices to others and rejected my claims to those offices". Sir George Arthur sent a copy of this letter, with his comments on the charges, to the colonial secretary, the Marquess of Normanby.[16]

In England, FitzGibbon got nowhere with his appeal. He was not granted an interview with the colonial secretary but only with the undersecretary. It happened that both Bishop Strachan and Chief Justice Robinson were in England that summer, and both wrote letters of support for him, copies of which FitzGibbon forwarded to the Colonial Office along with other documents. Robinson's letter, written to Strachan at the latter's request, was positive and explicit.

> During the many years that Colonel FitzGibbon has resided in Upper Canada, his resolute character, his ardent loyalty, and his active and intelligent mind, have led him, and have enabled him, to render important services to the Government and to the Province, and on several occasions when I think it would have been difficult to find any one else who could have discharged the same duty so efficiently.
>
> With regard to his service in 1837, I have no doubt, and I should be happy to state this on every occasion where it could be useful to him, that his earnest conviction before the outbreak that violence would be attempted, and the measures of precaution which he spontaneously took in consequence of that impression, were the means of saving the Government and the loyal inhabitants of Toronto from being for a time at least at the mercy of the Rebels; and I believe that the most disastrous consequences would have followed the surprise which Colonel FitzGibbon's vigilance prevented.[16]

The two testimonials failed to move the colonial secretary. It was made clear to FitzGibbon that the British government would not approve the bill to grant him the land, nor would it award him the value of the land in money.

(In the copy of Robinson's letter sent to the colonial secretary, FitzGibbon omitted two significant paragraphs in which the chief justice commented on the lieutenant-governor's action in reserving the 1839 land-grant bill. In these paragraphs, Robinson suggested that FitzGibbon's "highly excited feelings" which led him to look on the lieutenant-governor's action as "a personal injury to himself" were unjustified as His Excellency had acted only from his sense of duty. Robinson went on to say that he very much regretted FitzGibbon's act in leaving the province and he hoped that it would not prejudice his case).[17]

FitzGibbon's disappointing summer of 1839 in London yielded one happy result. He made a distinguished new friend in the person of Sir Augustus d'Este, to whom he had brought a letter of introduction from an officer in the Grenadier Guards. D'Este responded warmly and sympathetically to FitzGibbon's account of his difficulties. He seemed to recognize in the colonel a kindred spirit. Both men had served in the army (d'Este was a retired lieutenant-colonel on half pay) and both had experienced exceptional frustrations. Sir Augustus was the son of Augustus Frederick, Duke of Sussex, sixth son of George III. Prince Augustus had married Lady Augusta Murray, daughter of the Earl of Dunmore, by whom he had two children, Augustus Frederick and Ellen Augusta. King George had refused to recognize his son's marriage and forced the couple to separate. The Duke of Sussex was given custody of the children who adopted the name of "d'Este" from an old Italian princely family with whom they had an ancestral connection. Augustus d'Este was knighted by King William IV, Queen Victoria's uncle, and was also granted a pension, but he never succeeded in having his rights as a prince recognized. D'Este made a friendly gesture towards FitzGibbon by presenting him with an ornate sword that he had worn himself, and which he gave as a token of his belief in the colonel's worthiness. In subsequent years Sir Augustus used his influence in practical ways to help FitzGibbon win his reward.

Back in Upper Canada, FitzGibbon's sudden departure for England had given rise to doubts about his integrity. People wanted to know what had become of the money for contingent expenses (nearly £4,800) that had been credited to the clerk of the Assembly at the close of the parliamentary session, and why he had not paid the bills that his office owed. The postmaster, Charles Berczy, presented a bill for unpaid postage amounting to £947, and the government printer, Robert Stanton, claimed that he was suffering from financial embarrassment. Lieutenant-Governor Arthur asked FitzGibbon's assistant, William F. Patrick, to make an inquiry into the financial state of affairs in the Assembly clerk's office. Charles FitzGibbon, acting as his father's legal agent, declined to provide information on the funds, saying that the disposal of this money was under the control of the House of Assembly and it would be an infringement of its privileges to make a financial report to any other body. Since the

Assembly was not in session, Charles declared that he could not make a financial statement. When he tried at the end of June to collect his father's half-yearly salary, he was informed that the lieutenant-governor had given orders that it be withheld. Attorney-General Hagerman advised the Executive Council that, in his opinion, the process of law might be taken against FitzGibbon if he failed to account for the money in his charge. And so the discussions and correspondence on the situation dragged on from late May to the middle of September when it became known that FitzGibbon was on his way back home. He arrived on the second of October. No legal action was taken against him.

While still in England, FitzGibbon became uneasy about the effect his angry letter to Sir George Arthur might have on his career. He worried that he might be dismissed from his post as clerk of the Assembly. Before he sailed for Canada, he wrote apologetically to Sir George, expressing regret for his action in leaving the province without permission, and for the "very intemperate communication" which he had despatched from Montreal. As soon as he had returned to his office in Toronto he notified the lieutenant-governor, beseeching him to "overlook all that is past". Sir George Arthur did so, and allowed FitzGibbon to resume his duties as Assembly clerk.[18] In this post-rebellion period, political changes were taking place in Upper and Lower Canada that made settlement of FitzGibbon's reward increasingly difficult. FitzGibbon was disappointed repeatedly in his expectations. When Charles Poulett Thomson (later Baron Sydenham) came to Canada as governor general of the two provinces and, after the Act of Union, of the united Province of Canada, the Upper Canada House of Assembly raised the question of FitzGibbon's reward with him. He replied, as others had, that the 1839 bill was not consistent with the land act but he would be pleased to recommend a pecuniary reward. The House of Assembly then considered a resolution to pay FitzGibbon the sum of £2,500, but after acrimonious debate the motion was defeated. A bill repealing the limiting clause of the Public Lands Act was then introduced, but again Lieutenant-Governor Arthur reserved the bill.

With this setback, FitzGibbon turned to his former patron, Sir John Colborne, now Baron Seaton, asking him to use his influence to obtain the Queen's assent to the new bill, or, alternatively, the value of the land in money (£2,500). As recently as October 1839, Colborne had shown his interest in FitzGibbon by obtaining an ensign's commission for FitzGibbon's youngest son James, but he did not respond to FitzGibbon's impassioned plea of February 1840. A few months later, James wrote again, imploring Lord Seaton "to make some powerful effort in my behalf", and enclosing a copy of a memorial he had addressed recently to Lieutenant-Governor Arthur on the urgency of the matter. Seaton forwarded the correspondence to the colonial secretary, Lord John Russell, with a covering letter outlining FitzGibbon's services. Russell, like his predecessors, refused to sanction the grant of land, but declared himself agreeable to some other means of compensation. Colonel FitzGibbon thus went unrewarded for the fourth year.

There was one encouraging development. Lord Sydenham promoted FitzGibbon to the post of clerk of the Legislative Council of the Province of Canada at a salary of £450 (sterling) per year. For the time being, FitzGibbon also retained his old post as registrar of the Court of Probate, Upper Canada. But his finances continued to decline, as the change to union government caused a delay of several months in payment of £300 of his salary, as well as a lapse of four months between the expiration of his former post and the beginning of his new one, when he earned no salary but was entitled to a compensatory sum that remained unpaid for over a year. Just when his tide of fortune was at its lowest ebb, FitzGibbon's wife died (on 18 March 1841). At the time, he had only three dollars to his name, he said later, and if it had not been for an unexpected gift of £100, "I know not how I could have obtained money to defray the Expenses consequent on that Melancholy occasion". The gift came from Sir Augustus d'Este, who having learned of FitzGibbon's straitened circumstances (before Mary's death), "ventured to forward . . . a *Mite* from a *Brother Soldier* and a *friend*".[19]

The move of the union government from Toronto to

Kingston in 1841 further aggravated FitzGibbon's financial problems. He had to leave his house and other property behind and find new lodgings in Kingston. His creditors were pressing him and he was unable to meet their demands. When Robert Baldwin wrote to him on behalf of a legal client who was a creditor, FitzGibbon replied that he could not pay the debt. He had applied to the Commercial Bank for a loan of £200 but had been refused. He continued to hope that Parliament would grant his reward, but it was impossible to hasten action by the new Canadian government. It was a time of political adjustment, when English-speaking members of Parliament from Canada West (formerly Upper Canada) were learning to work with their counterparts, both English and French, from Canada East (Lower Canada). FitzGibbon found that members from the Eastern province did not understand his case, nor did they share the concern for him that was felt by members from old Upper Canada.

The sudden death of Lord Sydenham in September 1841, brought the wheels of government to an unexpected halt. Sydenham's successor, Sir Charles Bagot, an ailing man, did not arrive in Kingston until early the following year. In his two years of office, however, Bagot took an interest in FitzGibbon's case, generated by a petition that the latter addressed to him. Bagot urged the Executive Council to recommend the issue of land scrip to FitzGibbon for the sum of £2,000 but the Council decided against it. Sir Charles compensated FitzGibbon in some measure by extending patronage to two of his sons. He appointed Charles registrar of the Court of Probate in Canada West in place of his father, and named William clerk of the peace, Victoria District.

Meanwhile in England, Sir Augustus d'Este took steps to help FitzGibbon obtain his reward. He prepared a statement on FitzGibbon's services from material that the latter supplied.[20] He presented this statement personally to Lord Stanley, the colonial secretary, reading it aloud to him.

Stanley listened politely, but afterwards took no action. Next, d'Este exerted his influence on the newly-appointed Governor General of Canada, Sir Charles

Metcalfe. He chaired a dinner in honour of Metcalfe prior to the governor's departure from England. He followed this up the next day by calling on Metcalfe and presenting him with his statement on FitzGibbon's case. This made a favourable impression. From the beginning of his term of office, Governor General Metcalfe took a personal interest in FitzGibbon, and finally won for him his long-deferred reward.

But before that happened, FitzGibbon faced another financial crisis, his most serious one. By July 1842, his debts exceeded £3,000, a sum about six times his annual income. His creditors were threatening to sue him. Two notes for £75 each, owed to two different parties, were due, and one of the creditors started legal action. A third case involved more money — the Bank of Upper Canada threatened to take him to court for £250, the remainder of a £400 debt which he had partially paid. This action struck FitzGibbon as the ultimate in injustice. He wrote a scornful and almost hysterical letter to the bank's directors expressing his contempt for them: "You, whose Bank, containing £100,000 in gold and silver, I saved for you [in 1837], whose books and other evidences of debt I saved for you, which were worth to you £200,000 more, you drive me, already driven as I am almost to insanity". But, he said defiantly, "you dare not sue me in the face of the people of Upper Canada".[21] They did not sue him. FitzGibbon sold his Toronto house and his few remaining acres of land to pay the debt.

Early in 1843, FitzGibbon tried to persuade the Executive Council to advance him £500 on the assumption that the next session of Parliament would authorize the payment of his reward. The Council refused. Afterwards, Sir Charles Metcalfe, who had recently arrived in Canada, summoned FitzGibbon for an interview and questioned him about his financial situation. When the colonel told him that a baker had stopped providing bread for his family, Metcalfe offered to lend him money out of his own funds, and the next day he sent FitzGibbon a cheque for £200.

This gesture was characteristic of Metcalfe's generosity. He was an admirable and courageous man. While in Canada, he suffered from a fatal cancerous growth on his face, but carried on his duties conscientiously even while in great pain. As governor general, however, Canadian historians have criticized Metcalfe for resisting the trend to responsible government. He had formerly governed India and Jamaica, and he was accustomed to acting in an authoritarian way. He did not understand the strong urge towards self-government that the Canadians were experiencing and that would prove irresistible. Soon he became involved in a power struggle with the Executive Council that led to the dissolution of Parliament in November 1843.

This postponed any action that the Canadian government might take on behalf of FitzGibbon, but Metcalfe took other steps. When FitzGibbon impatiently addressed a petition to Queen Victoria, claiming that his services in 1837 had been rendered to the Empire quite as much as to the province of Upper Canada, the governor general withheld the petition until the Executive Council prepared a report that he requested on the colonel's case. The Council in its report recommended that a sum of money equivalent to the value of the land grant be paid to the colonel. The governor general then sent the petition to Lord Stanley with a covering letter in which he reviewed, most sympathetically, FitzGibbon's services and the circumstances of the delayed reward. Lord Stanley replied in April 1844 that the matter was in the hands of the Canadian Parliament.

By the time the 1844-45 session of Parliament opened, the seat of government had been transferred to Montreal. Early in 1845, Sir Charles Metcalfe sent a message to the Legislative Assembly recommending that it consider the question of FitzGibbon's reward. The colonel circularized the members of both Houses of the Legislature with information on his case. Finally, in March 1845, the reward was granted. What a disappointment it turned out to be! The sum of money was reduced to £1,000, less than half the amount of FitzGibbon's debts.

FitzGibbon failed to realize, or perhaps refused to face up to the reality, that public opinion on the rebellion had changed considerably since the Act of Union. The government had pardoned some of the rebels, such as David Gibson and John Montgomery in 1843, and Louis

Papineau in 1844. FitzGibbon was unwilling to accept his "unjust" reward without protest. He appealed over the next two years to various high government officials to have his reward augmented, but his appeals were unsuccessful. Two memorials to Queen Victoria were equally ineffective.

Unfortunately, James FitzGibbon became so obsessed with the pressure of his debts, his sense of the injustice done him, and his efforts to obtain redress, that he neglected his duties as clerk of the Legislative Council. He delayed moving to Montreal for several months after the capital had been transferred, and he repeatedly asked for leave of absence. He obtained medical certificates from two well-known doctors, who were old friends of his — Dr Christopher Widmer and Dr William Winder — stating, in effect, that he was mentally incapable of carrying out his duties because of his failed expectations and the exceptional distresses to which he had been subjected. The Legislative Council lost patience and took steps to force his resignation. It proposed to Lord Cathcart (who had succeeded Metcalfe), that His Excellency grant permission for the clerk to retire on pension. Lord Cathcart objected to the proposal, but the Legislative Council stood firm. It sent a message to Cathcart saying,

> We beg permission to inform Your Excellency, that the said James FitzGibbon, Esquire, is at present absent from this House without leave, and also that during the last four years he has altogether ceased to perform the duties of Clerk of this House, and has virtually transformed the Office into a sinecure, receiving the full amount of his salary without rendering therefor any service to this House, and entailing unnecessary expenses on the Country, which the recommendation of this House, if complied with, would reduce.[22]

The governor general acquiesced, and FitzGibbon was retired on an annual pension of £300 currency (£270 sterling), beginning on 15 July 1846.[23]

It was a sad exit for a man who had spent 30 years in the government service and 17 years before that in the British army. Except for the last few years of his career, he had been a conscientious and efficient public servant. He had given liberally of his time and energy, and had performed special services courageously and selflessly. He had run into debt out of the same spirit of generosity and boldness that had enabled him to carry out difficult assignments with skill and despatch. But he was now past the age of 65 and, according to the standards of his day, his pension was fair enough (three-fifths of his annual salary). Of course, FitzGibbon did not see it that way. His pride was hurt; his dismissal was humiliating in the extreme. "I am approaching a Crisis in my life", he wrote to Ferdinand Brock Tupper, in September 1846. (Tupper's biography of Brock, published the previous year, had led to a friendly correspondence between the author and FitzGibbon). "If no relief be afforded me in a short time I will go the Bar of the House of Commons and there cry aloud for justice", FitzGibbon continued. "Relief, or insanity or death, must soon be my lot".[24]

FitzGibbon did not suffer insanity, nor did he die for many years. He went to England in the fall of 1847 and never returned to Canada. FitzGibbon did not plan it that way. He intended to remain in England only long enough to persuade the British government to supplement his monetary reward, but the British authorities refused to recognize any "imperial" debt to him, and the Province of Canada considered his case closed.

Before he left Canada, FitzGibbon made one last effort to obtain from the province a sum of money more comparable to the reward promised in 1838. He published *An Appeal to the People of the Late Province of Upper Canada*, a 65-page pamphlet in which he reviewed his military and public services in Upper Canada and described the difficulties that had arisen over his reward. The pamphlet failed to bring any additional money but was successful in accomplishing another of FitzGibbon's purposes, to prepare "a defence against all future calumny". He explained:

> And now a question with me is whether I shall tamely sink into the grave under this fearful pressure [of debt] and leave my name and my character to be misrepresented by unjust men, who, having concealed my services, would malign my character to cover their own unworthiness, and their injustice, before I should thus make known to you [the people of Upper Canada] so much

> of the truth as I now state in this Appeal; and which Appeal I desire to leave behind me as a defence against all future calumny, should any appear against me.[25]

FitzGibbon's *Appeal* stands today as a worthy memorial of its author. Written in his lively and expressive style, the pamphlet, though poorly organized and admittedly biased, contains an extraordinary amount of information on what actually happened behind the scenes of government during the Upper Canadian Rebellion of 1837 and in the frustrating years while FitzGibbon waited for his reward. The author emerges from this highly personal record as a man of courage, determination and insight who was, at the same time, somewhat naive in his expectations. He was caught in the web of revolutionary events beyond his control and which he did not fully understand. His repeated disappointments combined with the weight of his debts almost unhinged his mind, as he himself said, and his obsession turned him into a querulous and embittered man. In England, he regained a measure of objectivity, and gradually his good spirits and healthy mind were restored.

King Henry VIII Gateway, main entrance to Windsor Castle

Chapter Nine

The Military Knight at Windsor Castle

"I begin to feel more strongly than before how incumbent it is upon me to bear patiently the pressure upon me .... And hitherto I have observed that with every one of my disappointments came some redeeming circumstances, which otherwise I could not have experienced". James FitzGibbon sent this surprisingly cheerful message to Ferdinand Brock Tupper (who lived in Guernsey) less than two months after his arrival in England.[1] He was living in cheap lodgings at 56 Stratford Place, London, not far from Buckingham Palace. As he led his lonely, frugal life, its monotony broken by visiting friends, reading, and walking in the park, FitzGibbon's thoughts must have turned frequently to the puzzling question: Why had he failed to achieve the degree of success he had sought in Upper Canada? We have no way of knowing what his conclusion was, but from the trend of his thinking in earlier letters and memorials we may suppose that his line of reasoning went somewhat as follows.

After the departure of Lieutenant-Governor Colborne, he had no patron to intercede for him, nor any powerful friends in the circle of advisers to Sir Francis Head or Sir George Arthur. On the contrary, he believed that the people close to the lieutenant-governors faulted him for his humble family background, his poor education, and his lack of gentlemanly attributes: manners, accomplishments, property. In short, they regarded him as an outsider. He was well aware that members of the

Family Compact were well educated, moderately wealthy, and conducted themselves with gentlemanly deportment. Many of them came from United Empire Loyalist stock. This assessment of his handicaps was factually true, but one questions if FitzGibbon saw the whole picture. Did he overlook certain other factors that may have contributed to his failure? There was, for instance, the example of William Allan, also an outsider, who succeeded nevertheless in becoming an influential member of the Family Compact. On the other hand, there was the contrasting example of Samuel Peters Jarvis, who was born and raised within the charmed circle of decision-makers but who failed, as FitzGibbon did, to rise to the position of power that he sought. A brief look at the careers of Allan and Jarvis may shed light on the viewpoint of the Family Compact and on the reasons why FitzGibbon was unable to penetrate its élite circle.

There were certain similarities between William Allan and James FitzGibbon. Both had come from the "old country". Both were poorly educated and lacked the background of gentlemen; both were conservative in outlook; both belonged to St James Anglican Church (Allan was treasurer), and both were distinguished veterans of the War of 1812. Allan, however, who was a militia officer, had the advantage of having worked closely with the Reverend John Strachan in the traumatic period following the surrender of York in 1813, when the two men cared for the wounded, helped to protect the civilians, and tried to ensure that the terms of surrender were observed. At that time also, Allan served as government agent in the Home District, a position that brought him to the attention of William Dummer Powell, then a judge of the Court of King's Bench and a man of influence in Upper Canada.

Even before the war, Allan had demonstrated his exceptional ability. He held several official positions — postmaster at York, customs collector, inspector of stills and taverns, and treasurer of the Home District — while at the same time he operated his own general store and wharf. After the war, he was appointed paymaster of militia claims, and in 1822 became the first president of the Bank of Upper Canada, possibly through the influence of John Strachan. Allan advanced steadily, becoming a board member of the Welland Canal Company (1825), commissioner of the Canada Company (1829), and first governor of the British American Life and Fire Insurance Company (1833). He was appointed to the Legislative Council in 1825 and the Executive Council in 1836.

It is clear that William Allan possessed talents of particular value to Upper Canada. In the crucial period when the province's commercial and financial institutions were developing, Allan's financial genius was recognized and he became indispensable to the government. James FitzGibbon had no such genius, nor did he have the prestigious friendship of a powerful insider like Bishop Strachan. Allan had the additional asset of being Scottish-born rather than Irish. The overweighing factor in his success, however, was his financial skill. FitzGibbon was rejected by the Family Compact not simply because he was an outsider, but because he lacked any special ability that might have made his services essential to the changing needs of the government. (His ability to quell riots was more in the nature of policing than of governing).

The case of Samuel Peters Jarvis was the opposite of William Allan's. Samuel was the son of William Jarvis, an officer who served in the Queen's Rangers with John Graves Simcoe, and who became the first provincial secretary and registrar of Upper Canada, a position that he held until his death in 1817. Samuel acted in that capacity during his father's illness, and hoped to succeed his father in the post. But the appointment went instead to Duncan Cameron, a Scottish-born merchant in York and a former aide-de-camp to Lieutenant-Governor Francis Gore.

Samuel Jarvis was educated by John Strachan, after which he trained in law and was called to the Bar in 1815. A few months before his father's death, Samuel fought a duel in which he killed John Ridout, son of Thomas Ridout, the surveyor-general of the province. In the subsequent trial, Jarvis was acquitted of the charge of murder, but his participation in the fatal duel may have spoiled his chance of becoming provincial secretary and registrar.

A year after the duel, Jarvis married Mary Boyles Powell, daughter of Chief Justice William Dummer Powell, a marriage that reinforced his position among the élite of Upper Canada. He had recently been appointed clerk of the Crown in chancery, and he retained that House of Assembly post until the union of the two Canadas. Jarvis reentered the office of the provincial secretary a few years later, and in 1827 was appointed deputy secretary and registrar even though he had rashly taken part in the destruction of Mackenzie's printing press the previous year. Jarvis' next appointment (in 1837) was that of chief superintendent of the Indian department.

When Duncan Cameron died in 1838 both Jarvis and FitzGibbon applied for the vacant post. In a memorial to Sir George Arthur, Jarvis explained why he wanted to become provincial secretary and registrar. His father had died in debt, he wrote, and it had fallen to him to relieve the distress of his father's family; he himself had eight children, and the difference in income between that of superintendent of the Indian department and that of provincial secretary (£250) would "indemnify" him for his difficulties. Jarvis indicated also that former lieutenant-governors had encouraged him to hope that he would be "strongly recommended" for the position of secretary and registrar when a vacancy should occur.[2] Sir George Arthur was not moved by the appeal of Jarvis any more than by that of FitzGibbon, and he carried out his intention of appointing R.A. Tucker to the post. Arthur's rejection of Jarvis' application meant for Samuel that he had reached his limit in the government service.

Jarvis found this finality hard to accept. Seven years later he was forced to retire from his Indian department post because of maladministration (due partly, at least, to his demoralized state following his rejection for the post he wanted). Thus his career was brought to an end for reasons very similar to those that caused James FitzGibbon's dismissal from his position with the Legislative Council. More significantly, both men lacked an outstanding ability that might have led to the status that each sought. In the competitive world of preferment in Upper Canada, Jarvis' privileged birth and education proved to be of limited advantage to him.

As for FitzGibbon, the special relationship that he had enjoyed with two lieutenant-governors propelled him only so far. Afterwards, when he believed that the special services he had performed for the province (quelling riots, winning the victory at Beaver Dams, and leading the attack against the rebels in 1837) should entitle him to a position in the higher echelons of government, he found that neither the lieutenant-governors nor their Family Compact advisers concurred with his view. No doubt the Family Compact tended to favour members of its own circle in recommendations for government appointments, but its leaders were concerned also about the ability of candidates. The men at the centre, such as Bishop Strachan and John Beverley Robinson, were noted for their intelligence and ability as well as for their privileged positions of power.

Whatever conclusions James FitzGibbon may have reached regarding his failure, his thoughts soon turned away from brooding over his disappointments. Within a year after his arrival in England, he began writing on a subject that was not remotely connected with the government or public service of Upper Canada. The subject was child training. Under the pseudonym "A Colonist", FitzGibbon wrote *Remarks on the Advantages of Early Training and Management of Children*, a pamphlet that was published in London by John Ollivier in 1848. FitzGibbon put forth the argument that the earliest years in a child's life were of special importance in the development of that child, a belief that is commonly held today. "What you wish a child to be, be that to the child", he stated. FitzGibbon's surprising interest in the training of infants and children was, he told Tupper, "a subject to which, for more than 50 years, I have devoted more of my thoughts and observations than even to my military duties".[3] His pamphlet attracted the attention of the celebrated British author, Harriet Martineau, who quoted extracts from it in her book, *Household Education*, a popular book that ran to several editions.[4] Besides his pamphlet, James wrote some articles on infant training that appeared in Ollivier's magazine, *Home Circle*.

FitzGibbon had been introduced to John Ollivier by Jane Strickland, one of three literary sisters who were friends of his. Each of the Strickland sisters — Elizabeth, Agnes and Jane — were well-known authors in their day. (A fourth sister, Sara, who lived also in England, was not a writer.) Elizabeth Strickland, the eldest of the sisters, had a cottage in Bayswater, London, where James visited from time to time. She had edited the *Court Magazine*, after which she contributed many of the biographies that formed part of the popular series, *Lives of the Queens of England*, compiled by her sister Agnes. Agnes was a prolific author of historical tales and biographies. The third sister, Jane, though less prolific than Agnes, also wrote books on historical themes, most notably *Rome, Regal and Republican, a Family History of Rome.* Jane Strickland and FitzGibbon were particularly warm friends. Like Anna Jameson, Jane found in FitzGibbon a unique personality and a storyteller of great charm. She said of him, "He was plain [plain-spoken], decidedly plain, but he carried himself well, was a fine-looking man, and the moment he began to talk, all else was forgotten".[5] There was a Canadian connection with the Stricklands. The two youngest sisters in the family (as well as a brother, Samuel) lived in Canada, and they are known today for their books on pioneer life and other subjects. Catherine Parr Traill, author of *The Backwoods of Canada*, lived near Peterborough. The youngest sister, Susanna Moodie, best known for her classic, *Roughing It in the Bush*, lived, at this period, in Belleville. Her husband John W. Dunbar Moodie was the sheriff of the Victoria District, afterwards of Hastings county. James FitzGibbon had become friends with the Moodies when visiting his son William, who moved to Belleville after he became clerk of the peace, Victoria District. The friendship between the FitzGibbons and the Moodies was strengthened by the bond of marriage, in 1850, between Charles FitzGibbon and Agnes Dunbar Moodie, daughter of Susanna and John. Agnes Moodie was a gifted artist. In later years she illustrated two books by her nature-loving aunt, Mrs Traill: *Canadian Wild Flowers* (1868), and *Studies of Plant Life in Canada* (1885). In the third generation, Mary Agnes FitzGibbon, daughter of Charles and Agnes, carried on the literary tradition. She wrote the first biography of her grandfather, *A Veteran of 1812, the Life of James FitzGibbon* (1894).

In London, James soon exhausted his interest in writing about the upbringing of children. He turned to the Canadian political scene for his next pamphlet, *A Few Observations on Canada and the Other Provinces of British North America*, which he intended for British readers. FitzGibbon dealt at length with the military power of the United States and its danger for Canada, but the views he expressed in "Memorandum on . . . Canadian Affairs" are of more interest to the reader of today. This section was basically the same as his paper for Lord Durham in 1838. He maintained that a federation of all the British North American provinces would be preferable to union between Upper and Lower Canada because federation would ensure the predominance of the "British race". He protested that "I have no idea of treating the Canadians of French descent, after such union, as not fully entitled to equal privileges and advantages of every description as their other fellow-subjects in Lower Canada. From my long acquaintance with their social virtues and amiable qualities I respect and love them".[6] In expressing this sentiment, FitzGibbon was quite sincere, but like many other Britishers of his time he firmly believed in the right of the British to rule.

James had hoped that he would be able to find employment in England. He failed, but was fortunate in having a good friend, the former lieutenant-governor, Sir John Colborne, now Lord Seaton. Through his efforts, Colonel FitzGibbon was admitted to the order of the Military Knights of Windsor, and on 12 June 1850 he took up residence at Windsor Castle. There he lived in one of the small stone houses reserved for the military knights in the Lower Ward directly across from St George's Chapel.

FitzGibbon was one of 18 veteran army officers who lived there on the Queen's bounty, all selected on the basis of financial need and distinguished military service. The order dates back to the fourteenth century when King Edward III founded the Order of the Garter and made provision at the same time for a certain number of impoverished warriors or "poor knights" to be supported from Crown revenue. Besides free housing, the military knights received a small allowance, a shilling a day when FitzGibbon entered the order. In keeping with military tradition, the knights wore a colourful uniform, distinguished by a scarlet coat trimmed with gilt buttons and

Stone cottages, Military Knights of Windsor, Windsor Castle, showing pillars at entrance to each cottage

gold epaulettes. A cocked hat with white feathers completed the costume. At his side, each knight carried a curved sword in a black leather scabbard with gilt mountings.

Most of the knights were married and their wives lived with them and kept house for them just as they had in their own private homes. Mary FitzGibbon and her cousin Margaret joined James soon after he moved to Windsor Castle. Unfortunately, the colonel's early years in Windsor Castle were saddened by the deaths of three of his family. William was the first to go. He visited his father in Windsor Castle, hoping that the sea voyage to England and the change of air would restore his failing health, but he did not recover. William died at his own home in Belleville in 1851, aged 32.

Mary FitzGibbon was especially dear to her father but she too was in declining health. A doctor recommended that she drink goat's milk, and her devoted father walked six miles every other day to bring her milk from the goats on a farm in the park, owned by Prince Albert. The milk failed to work a magic cure. James decided to take Mary to Dublin, thinking she would receive better care in his brother's house than he could give her at Windsor. This cure also failed. Mary died in Dublin in July 1852, and was buried beside her grandparents in the cemetery of St Matthews Church, Irishtown, Dublin. She was 36. Meanwhile, 31-year-old James Gerald, the youngest member of the family, had died earlier that year in Belleville, (Charles FitzGibbon, the only one of the family to survive his father, lived to be 47). Margaret FitzGibbon, the niece who had lived with the FitzGibbons in Canada, stayed with her uncle at Windsor Castle and cared for him as long as he lived.

FitzGibbon was not long installed at Windsor Castle before he was elected chairman of a knights' committee to pursue the question of a larger allowance with the dean and canons of Windsor, the officials who were responsible for the welfare of the military knights. The committee learned that the revenue from lands set aside by King Henry VIII for the benefit of the knights had increased from £600 per year to £15,000, without any corresponding increase in the knights' allowance. Colonel FitzGibbon,

Colonel James FitzGibbon in uniform of Military Knight of Windsor

as committee chairman, wrote and talked to many prominent men, soliciting their support for the military knights and seeking their advice. The case was discussed in the British Parliament and was brought before the courts. Finally, after a ten-year battle, a victory of sorts was achieved. Parliament passed an act that trebled the income of the military knights. It was not as much as the committee had requested, nor as much as the knights thought they were entitled to, but the chairman and his fellows at Windsor Castle considered that the struggle had been well worthwhile.

FitzGibbon's debts continued to worry him. He used the greater part of his Canadian pension to pay them off gradually. At last, only £60 remained. This amount he owed to his brother Gerald, a prominent lawyer in Dublin who later became the receiver-master in chancery for Ireland. Gerald had sent James £1,000, some time before the latter had left Canada, to enable him to reduce his debts. When Gerald saw that the worry over the last £60 was affecting the health of his aging brother, then in his mid-seventies, he cancelled the debt.

Thus, as FitzGibbon grew older, his life at Windsor Castle became more peaceful. He enjoyed taking long walks in the surrounding park, going to London to visit his friends, and entertaining those who called on him at Windsor. He read a great deal and wrote letters to his friends and the newspapers. The military knights were expected to attend services at St George's Chapel every day, and Colonel FitzGibbon observed this duty conscientiously.

Friends from Canada sometimes visited him. One of them, the Reverend Henry Scadding of Toronto, left the following memorable picture of the old colonel.

> Though most romantically ensconced and very comfortably lodged within the walls of the noblest of all the royal residences of Europe, his [FitzGibbon's] heart, we found, was far away, ever recurring to the scenes of old activities. Where the light streamed in through what seemed properly an embrasure for cannon, pierced through a wall several yards in thickness, we saw a pile of Canadian newspapers. To pore over these was his favourite occupation.

> After chatting with him in his room, we went with him to attend Divine Service in the magnificent Chapel of St George close by. We then strolled together round the ramparts of the Castle, enjoying the incomparable views. Since the time of William IV the habit of the Military Knights is that of an officer of high rank in full dress, cocked hat and feather included. As our venerable friend passed the several sentries placed at intervals about the Castle, arms were duly presented, an attention which each time elicited from the Colonel the words, rapidly interposed in the midst of a stream of earnest talk, and accompanied by deprecatory gestures of the hand, "Never mind *me*, boy! Never mind *me*!"[7]

When he was 79, James FitzGibbon suffered an apopletic seizure. He recovered from the attack, and although he never regained his old vigour, his brain remained undamaged. A year after his stroke, he wrote a remarkable letter to *The London Review and Weekly Journal of Politics, Literature, Art & Society.* His letter was published on 21 July 1860 under the heading "The History of a Life", and signed "An Old Soldier". FitzGibbon introduced himself by saying, "I am in the eightieth year of my age, feeble in body, but with mind still active, and ever looking intently on passing events, whether religious, political, or social". He related memories of his childhood, told of his intense interest in reading even as a small child, described how Colonel Brock had shamed him into studying English grammar, and how he had learned to manage the soldiers under his command by treating them "as a lady would her piano". He went on to express his belief in the value of education for everyone, not just for the privileged few. "The efforts that many make to prevent or delay the increase of knowledge among the masses are producing, and will more and more produce, the most unhappy results . . . . Let the upper classes be not so much afraid of enlarging the minds of the masses". (Compulsory education in Great Britain was still 16 years in the future). FitzGibbon closed his letter with an affirmation of his religious creed: "Love the Lord your God with all your heart, with all your mind, and with all your strength, and your neighbour as yourself". Without this creed, he

Memorial to Military Knights of Windsor buried in the crypt at Windsor Castle

said, "I know not how I could have happiness here, or hope for any hereafter".[8]

James FitzGibbon had survived the struggles and frustrations of his life, and he had finally conquered the bitterness and resentment that nearly ruined him. He died at Windsor Castle on 10 December 1863, not long after his eighty-third birthday. He was buried in the crypt of St George's Chapel. His death attracted little attention in Canada, only a two-line notice in a Toronto newspaper.[9]

Notes

Abbreviations

AO	Archives of Ontario
MTL	Metropolitan Toronto Library
PAC	Public Archives Canada
WCHS	Women's Canadian Historical Society of Toronto

Chapter 1

1. *Colonial Advocate* (Toronto), 6 Oct. 1831.
2. PAC, MG 11, Q series (Transcripts of Colonial Office Records), vol. 376, pt. 2, p. 449, Mr. Mackenzie's Letters, Petitions, &c., 1832.

Chapter 2

1. AO, F.B. Tupper Papers, James FitzGibbon to F.B. Tupper, 12 Sept. 1846.
2. *Ibid.*
3. *Ibid.*
4. PAC, RG 8, C series (Military Documents), vol. 924, p. 24, FitzGibbon to Vincent, 16 May 1812.

Chapter 3

1. F.B. Tupper, ed., *The Life and Correspondence of Major-General Sir Isaac Brock, K.B.* (London, Simpkin, Marshall & Co., 2d. ed., 1847), pp. 352-53.
2. Wentworth Historical Society, *Journals and Transactions* (Hamilton, 1892), vol. 1, p. 23.
3. AO, Plenderleath Papers, 1912-1914, Misc. 1912, FitzGibbon to James Somerville, 7 June 1813.
4. AO, F.B. Tupper Papers, FitzGibbon to Tupper, 25 June 1848.
5. PAC, MG 29, D61 (H.J. Morgan Papers), vol. 7 (James FitzGibbon), p. 3000.
6. PAC, RG 8, C series, vol. 1227, pp. 180-81, "Extract from the Instructions issued by Lt. Colonel Harvey, Dy. Adj't Gen'l to Lieut. FitzGibbon . . . 17 June 1813".
7. [Cyrenius Chapin], *Chapin's Review of Armstrong's Notices of the War of 1812* (Black Rock, U.S.A., D.P. Adams, 1836), p. 10.
8. *Niles' Weekly Register* (Baltimore, U.S.A.), vol. 10 (20 April 1816), p. 119, "Battle of the Beaver Dams".
9. [Charles] Boerstler, "Narrative of the Expedition from Fort George to the Beaver Dams, U.C.", in John Armstrong, *Notices of the War of 1812* (2 vols., New York, 1836), vol. 1, Appendix 24; reprinted in E.A. Cruikshank, *Documentary History of the Campaign upon the Niagara Frontier* (9 vols., Welland, Ont., Lundy's Lane Historical Society, 1896-1908), vol. 4, pp. 130-37, quotation, 133-34.
10. AO, F.B. Tupper Papers, FitzGibbon to Tupper, 26 Nov. 1845; M.A. FitzGibbon, *A Veteran of 1812, the Life of James FitzGibbon* (Toronto, William Briggs, 1894), pp. 89-91.
11. PAC, RG 5, A1 (Upper Canada Sundries), vol. 84, pp. 45661-62, dated York, 11 May 1827; vol. 46, p. 22847, 1820 certificate; RG 5, C1 (Provincial Secretary's Office, C.W.), vol. 82, no. 2880, 1837 certificate enclosed. The three certificates are printed in full in Ruth McKenzie, *Laura Secord, the Legend and the Lady* (Toronto, McClelland and Stewart, 1971), pp. 90, 125, 128-29.
12. Boerstler's "Narrative of the Expedition", as in Cruikshank, *Documentary History*, vol. 4, p. 130.

13. PAC, RG 8, C series, vol. 679, pt. 1, p. 140, FitzGibbon to De Haren, 24 June 1813.
14. WCHS, FitzGibbon Papers, FitzGibbon to Somerville, 24 June 1813. (A copy of these papers is in AO.)
15. Private collection, FitzGibbon Papers, Baldwin to FitzGibbon, 30 March 1836.
16. PAC, RG 8, C series, vol. 1170, p. 281, General Order; vol. 1227, p. 182, Prevost to FitzGibbon, 29 June 1813.
17. PAC, RG 5, A1, vol. 97, p. 54453, FitzGibbon to Kerr, 30 March 1818.
18. PAC, RG 8, C series, vol. 679, pp. 132-34, Bisshopp to Vincent, 24 June 1813.
19. For a description of Laura Secord's walk, based on documentary evidence, *see* Ruth McKenzie, *Laura Secord, the Legend and the Lady*, chapter 5.

Chapter 4

1. Anna B. Jameson, *Winter Studies and Summer Rambles in Canada* (3 vols., London, Saunders and Otley, 1838), vol. 1, p. 131.
2. PAC, RG 9, I, B1 (Militia Adjutant General's Office, Upper Canada), Letter Book, 1812-1823, Coffin to Major Hillier, secretary to Lieutenant-Governor Maitland, 29 Aug. 1818.
3. PAC, MG 29, D61, vol. 7, pp. 2994-95.
4. PAC, RG 5, A1, vol. 39, pp. 18350-51, Brock to Maitland, 30 April 1818.
5. *Upper Canada Gazette and Weekly Register* (York), 25 April 1822, as reprinted in E.G. Firth, ed., *Town of York, 1815-1834* (Toronto, The Champlain Society, 1966), pp. 308-10.
6. James FitzGibbon, *An Appeal to the People of the Late Province of Upper Canada* (Montreal, Lovell and Gibson, 1847), p. 7.
7. PAC, RG 5, A1, vol. 60, pp. 31450-51, FitzGibbon to Maitland, 2 April 1823.
8. Henry Scadding, *Toronto of Old*, abr. and ed. by F.H. Armstrong (Toronto, Oxford University Press, 1966), pp. 81, 251.
9. J.R. Robertson, *The History of Freemasonry in Canada from Its Introduction in 1749 . . . .* (2 vols., Toronto, Morang, 1899), vol. 2, pp. 64-65.
10. PAC, MG 11, Q series, vol. 336, pt. 1, pp. 137-41, J.H. Powell (and 14 Justices of the Peace) to Hillier, 4 May 1824.
11. PAC, MG 20, D61, vol. 7, p. 3003.
12. *Ibid.*, p. 3004.
13. PAC, MG 11, Q series, vol. 336, pt. 1, pp. 157-69, FitzGibbon to Hillier, 10 June 1824.
14. PAC, RG 5, A1, vol. 67, pp. 35275-77, FitzGibbon to Baines, 4 June 1824.
15. PAC, MG 11, Q series, vol. 168, pt. 1, pp. 169-70, Dalhousie to Bathurst, 18 May 1824; vol. 336, pt. 1, pp. 134-36, Maitland to Bathurst, 27 July 1824.
16. A reference to Maitland's travels to and from his estate, Stamford Park, not far from Queenston.
17. PAC, RG 5, A1, vol. 76, pp. 40938-41, FitzGibbon to unknown informant, 23 Feb. 1826; Z. Burnham to FitzGibbon, 3 March 1826.
18. J.C. Dent, *The Story of the Upper Canadian Rebellion* (2 vols., Toronto, C. Blackett Robinson, 1885), vol. 1, pp. 138-40.
19. PAC, RG 5, A1, vol. 87, pp. 47685-88, Statement by FitzGibbon, 14 Jan. 1828.

Chapter 5

1. PAC, RG 5, A1, vol. 87, p. 47725, FitzGibbon to Hillier, 17 Jan. 1828.

2. *Canadian Freeman* (York), 15 July 1830.
3. FitzGibbon, *An Appeal to the People*, p. 63, quoting a letter from FitzGibbon to Major Campbell, 21 May 1847.
4. PAC, RG 5, A1, vol. 78, pp. 41932-34, "To the Orangemen of Cavan and Perth", 18 June 1826.
5. *Canadian Freeman*, 15 July 1830.
6. *Ibid.*, 22 July 1830, reprinted from the *York Observer*.
7. PAC, RG 5, A1, vol. 100, pp. 56370-71, FitzGibbon to Mudge, 11 May 1830.
8. *Ibid.*, vol. 101, pp. 57024-26, FitzGibbon to Mudge, 7 July 1830.
9. PAC, MG 29, D61, vol. 7, pp. 3004-05.
10. *Ibid.*, p. 3006.
11. PAC, MG 11, Q series, vol. 374, pt. 4, pp. 813-15, Colborne to Goderich, 11 July 1832.
12. PAC, RG 5, A1, vol. 166, pp. 90527-28, Memorial of FitzGibbon to Head, 6 May 1836.
13. *Ibid.*, vol. 117, pp. 65533-36, Memorial of FitzGibbon to Colborne, 4 June 1832.
14. *Colonial Advocate*, 18 July 1833.
15. *The Patriot* (York), 19 July 1833; *Colonial Advocate*, 18 July 1833.
16. PAC, MG 11, Q series, vol. 376, pt. 2, pp. 350, 449,, 461, 465, 467-68, copied from the *Colonial Advocate*, Sept. and Oct. 1831.

Chapter 6

1. Dent, *Upper Canadian Rebellion*, vol. 1, p. 138.
2. Scadding, *Toronto of Old*, p. 250.
3. M.A. FitzGibbon, *A Veteran of 1812*, pp. 175-76.
4. PAC, RG 5, A1, vol. 166, p. 90532, Rowan to FitzGibbon, 20 Jan. 1836.
5. PAC, MG 11, Q series, vol. 430, pt. 4, p. 717, Seaton to Russell, 6 Aug. 1840.
6. A. Ewart and J. Jarvis, "The Personnel of the Family Compact, 1791-1841", *Canadian Historical Review*, vol. 7 (Sept. 1926), pp. 211-15; R.E. Saunders, "What Was the Family Compact?", *Ontario History*, vol. 49 (Autumn, 1957), pp. 165-78.
7. PAC, RG 5, A1, vol. 162, pp. 88691-93, FitzGibbon to Joseph, 22 Feb. 1836.
8. *Ibid.*, vol. 166, pp. 90524-31, Memorial of FitzGibbon to Head, 6 May 1836; 90557-58, FitzGibbon to Joseph, 6 May 1836.
9. PAC, RG 7, G16, C (Civil Secretary's Letter Book), vol. 36, pp. 165-66, Joseph to FitzGibbon, 18 June 1836.
10. PAC, RG 5, A1, vol. 167, pp. 91525-26, 91541-44, FitzGibbon to Joseph, 24, 26 June 1836.
11. *Ibid.*, pp. 91584-86, 91616-19, FitzGibbon to Joseph, 29, 30 June 1836.
12. *Ibid.*, vol. 168, pp. 91738-43 FitzGibbon to Joseph, 6 July 1836.
13. *Ibid.*, vol. 205, pp. 113624-26, FitzGibbon to Head, 15 Oct. 1836.
14. Jameson, *Winter Studies and Summer Rambles*, vol. 1, pp. viii-ix, 98, 128-34.

Chapter 7

1. Charles Lindsey, *The Life and Times of Wm. Lyon Mackenzie* . . . (2 vols., Toronto, P.R. Randall, 1862), vol. 1, p. 382.
2. PAC, MG 11, Q series, vol. 391, p. 226, Sir F.B. Head, "Memorandum on the present political State of the Canadas", 28 Oct. 1836.
3. *Ibid.*, vol. 398, pt. 3, p. 649, Head to Colborne, 31 Oct. 1837.
4. MTL, James FitzGibbon, "Narrative of Occurrences in Toronto, Upper Canada in December, 1837" (Toronto, 13 Dec. 1837), pp. 1-2.
5. FitzGibbon, *An Appeal to the People*, p. 11.

6. PAC, MG 24, A40 (Colborne Papers), vol. 10, p. 2834, Robinson to Head, 1 Nov. 1837.
7. AO, Ms 78 (Macaulay Papers), J. Macaulay to Ann Macaulay, 30 Oct. 1837; Egerton Ryerson, *The Story of My Life* (Toronto, William Briggs, 1883), p. 176.
8. Lindsey, *Wm. Lyon Mackenzie*, vol. 2, pp. 358-62, Appendix F.
9. FitzGibbon, *An Appeal to the People*, p. 12; MTL, FitzGibbon, "Narrative of Occurrences in Toronto", p. 3.
10. On the identity of Mr. L., *see* J.S. Moir, "FitzGibbon's Secret Visitor", *Ontario History*, vol. 48 (Summer, 1956), pp. 108-10.
11. FitzGibbon, *An Appeal to the People*, pp. 13-14.
12. MTL, FitzGibbon, "Narrative of Occurrences in Toronto", pp. 4-5.
13. FitzGibbon, *An Appeal to the People*, pp. 15-16; MTL, FitzGibbon, "Narrative of Occurrences in Toronto", pp. 6-7.
14. [W.L. Mackenzie], *Mackenzie's Own Narrative of the Rebellion . . . in the Month of December 1837* (Toronto, Palladium Office, 1838), pp. 12-14; *The Patriot*, 16 Feb. 1838, narrative by John Powell.
15. FitzGibbon, *An Appeal to the People*, p. 18; MTL, FitzGibbon, "Narrative of Occurrences in Toronto", p. 8.
16. Lindsey, *Wm. Lyon Mackenzie*, vol. 2, pp. 81-82.
17. FitzGibbon, *An Appeal to the People*, pp. 18-19.
18. *Ibid.*, pp. 24-26; MTL, FitzGibbon, "Narrative of Occurrences in Toronto", pp. 10-13.
19. Sir F.B. Head, *The Emigrant* (New York, Harper, 1847), pp. 110-11.
20. FitzGibbon, *An Appeal to the People*, pp. 26-27; MTL, FitzGibbon, "Narrative of Occurrences in Toronto", p. 14-16, long quotation, p. 15.
21. MTL, FitzGibbon, "Narrative of Occurrences in Toronto", p. 16; Head, *The Emigrant*, pp. 112-14.
22. FitzGibbon, *An Appeal to the People*, pp. 28-30; MTL, FitzGibbon, "Narrative of Occurrences in Toronto", pp. 17-18.

Chapter 8

1. MTL, FitzGibbon, "Narrative of Occurrences in Toronto", p. 18.
2. PAC, MG 24, A 40, vol. 13, p. 3788, Foster to Colborne, 24 Jan. 1838; MTL, FitzGibbon, "Narrative of Occurrences in Toronto", p. 19.
3. PAC, RG 5, A1, vol. 205, pp. 113618-19, FitzGibbon to Head, 12 Dec. 1837.
4. PAC, MG 11, Q series, vol. 398, pt. 2, pp. 436-38, "Extract of a Despatch from Lieutenant-Governor Sir F.B. Head, Bart. to Lord Glenelg, dated Toronto, 19 December 1837".
5. Upper Canada, Legislative Council, *Journal*, 3d session. 13th Parlt., 1838, Appendix F, p. 26.
6. FitzGibbon, *An Appeal to the People*, p. 32.
7. PAC, RG 5, A1, vol. 194, p. 108279, "Testimonial to Colonel FitzGibbon".
8. *Ibid.*, pp. 108276-80, Thomas Galt, Sec., to J. Joseph, 30 May 1838; John Powell, Mayor (and committee members) to Sir George Arthur, 29 May 1838, enclosing printed copy of "Testimonial to Colonel FitzGibbon".
9. PAC, RG 4, B51 (Colonel James FitzGibbon's Claims, 1839-1846), vol. 1, unp., "Note referring to Chief Justice Robinson's Letter to the Bishop of Toronto. . . ."
10. PAC, MG 24, A27 (Durham Papers), vol. 26, pp. 659-67, James FitzGibbon, "Observations on the Canadas", dated 18, 20, 26 June 1838.
11. PAC, RG 5, A1, vol. 201, pp. 11381-88, FitzGibbon to Glenelg, 9 Aug. 1838. Copy also in PAC, MG 24, A27, vol. 27, pp. 76-84, dated 10 Aug. 1838.

12. PAC, MG 11, Q series, vol. 408, pt. 1, pp. 170-71, Arthur to Glenelg, 29 Sept. 1838; 174-78, encl. FitzGibbon to Glenelg, 24 Sept. 1838.
13. *Ibid.*, vol. 417, pt. 2, pp. 446-47, FitzGibbon to Arthur, 11 March 1839.
14. PAC, RG 5, A1, vol. 201, p. 111385, FitzGibbon to Glenelg, 9 Aug. 1839.
15. PAC, MG 11, Q series, vol. 417, pt. 2, p. 434, FitzGibbon to Arthur, 25 May 1839, with "Sir Geo. Arthur's Remarks thereon".
16. *Ibid.*, pp. 431-45.
17. FitzGibbon, *An Appeal to the People,* pp. 37-38; the complete letters in PAC, MG 24, A40, vol. 23, pp. 6990-91, Robinson to Strachan, 14 Aug. 1839, Strachan to FitzGibbon, 16 Aug. 1839.
18. PAC, RG 5, A1, vol. 227, pp. 124277-78, FitzGibbon to Arthur, 23 Aug. 1839; vol. 230, pp. 126333-34, FitzGibbon to Arthur, 8 Oct. 1839.
19. PAC, MG 24, A13 (Bagot Papers), vol. 6, pp. 289-90, FitzGibbon to Sir Charles Bagot, 18 April 1842; PAC, MG 29, D61, vol. 7, pp. 2980-84A, d'Este to FitzGibbon, 8 Feb. 1841.
20. Published as *Documents, Selected from Several Others, Showing the Services Rendered by Colonel FitzGibbon, while Serving in Upper Canada, between the Years 1812 and 1837* (Windsor, England, 1859).
21. FitzGibbon, *An Appeal to the People*, pp. 45-46, FitzGibbon to the Directors, Bank of Upper Canada, 6 April 1843.
22. Province of Canada, Legislative Council, *Journal*, 1846, pp. 134, 183, 186-87.
23. *Ibid.*, pp. 199, 205-06, 211; PAC RG 1, E 13 (Blue Books, Province of Canada), vol. 22, 1846, p. 216.
24. AO, F.B. Tupper Papers, FitzGibbon to Tupper, 12 Sept. 1846.
25. FitzGibbon, *An Appeal to the People* (Montreal, Lovell and Gibson, 1847), p. 48.

Chapter 9

1. AO, F.B. Tupper Papers, FitzGibbon to Tupper, 30 Nov. 1847.
2. PAC, MG 11, Q series, vol. 408, pt. 1, pp. 209-13, Memorial of Jarvis to Arthur, 12 Sept. 1838.
3. AO, F.B. Tupper Papers, FitzGibbon to Tupper, 25 Jan. 1848.
4. Harriet Martineau, *Household Education* (London, 1849, rev. ed., 1867), extracts from FitzGibbon's pamphlet, pp. 2, 247-48.
5. M. A. FitzGibbon, *A Veteran of 1812*, p. 266.
6. PAC, RG 8, C series, vol. 1711, pp. 123-35, quotation, 125-26. Published in London by John Ollivier, 1849, reprinted in Windsor, 1855. The idea of a federation of all the provinces was not original with FitzGibbon. John Strachan had proposed it as early as 1822.
7. Scadding, *Toronto of Old*, pp. 251-52.
8. The letter was reprinted in H.J. Morgan, *Sketches of Celebrated Canadians* .... (Quebec, Hunter, Rose, 1862), pp. 192-96.
9. *Daily Leader* (Toronto), 7 Jan. 1864.

Illustration and Photograph Credits

Page 6, from J.R. Robertson, *The History of Freemasonry in Canada from its Introduction in 1749 . . . Vol. 2 Courtesy Baldwin Room, Metropolitan Toronto Library*
Page 12, R. McKenzie, 1973
Page 22, No. C 11222, Public Archives Canada
Page 31, Public Archives Canada
Page 36, No. C 10717, Public Archives Canada
Page 47, courtesy Metropolitan Toronto Library
Page 53, No. C 5461, Public Archives Canada
Page 73, No. C 20764, Public Archives Canada
Page 82, courtesy Metropolitan Toronto Library
Page 98, No. C 18789, Public Archives Canada
Page 108, from the lithograph by R.J. Lane, after the painting by H.P. Briggs, R.A.
Page 112, No. C 105847, Public Archives Canada
Page 118, courtesy Metropolitan Toronto Library
Page 124, No. C 3918, Public Archives Canada
Page 131, No. C 13988, Public Archives Canada
Page 145, courtesy Metropolitan Toronto Library
Page 166, R. McKenzie, 1973
Page 174, R. McKenzie, 1973
Page 176, No. C 105846, Public Archives Canada
Page 179, R. McKenzie, 1973

Selected Bibliography

Manuscript Sources

Archives of Ontario: Macaulay Papers, Ms 78.
Plenderleath Papers, 1912-1914, Misc. 1912.
F.B. Tupper Papers, 1804-1850.

Metropolitan Toronto Library: James FitzGibbon, "Narrative of Occurrences in Toronto, Upper Canada in December 1837". Toronto, 13 Dec. 1837.

Private Collection: FitzGibbon Papers

Public Archives of Canada:
MG 11, CO 42 (Colonial Office records).
MG 11, CO 47 (Blue Books of Statistics, Upper Canada and Province of Canada).
MG 11, Q series (Colonial Office records, Transcripts).
MG 24, A40 (Sir John Colborne Papers).
MG 29, D61 (H.J. Morgan Papers), vol. 7 (James FitzGibbon).
RG 1, E13 (Blue Books of Statistics, Upper Canada and Province of Canada).
RG 4, B51 (Colonel James FitzGibbon's Claims, 1839-1846).
RG 5, A1 (Upper Canada Sundries).
RG 8, C series (Military documents).
RG 9, I, B1 (Militia Adjutant General's Office, Upper Canada).
RG 9, I, B3 (Militia General Orders).

Women's Canadian Historical Society of Toronto:
FitzGibbon Papers (Copies in Archives of Ontario).

Publications and Dissertations

Aitchison, J.H. "The Development of Local Government in Upper Canada 1783-1850", Ph.D. diss., University of Toronto, 1953.

Armstrong, F.H. "The York Riots of March 23, 1832", *Ontario History*, 55 (June 1963), 61-72.

"Battle of the Beaver Dams", *Niles Weekly Register* (Baltimore, U.S.A.), 10 (20 April 1816), 119-21.

Burns, R.J. "God's Chosen People: the Origins of Toronto Society, 1793-1818", Canadian Historical Association *Historical Papers 1973*, 213-28.

[Chapin, Cyrenius]. *Chapin's Review of Armstrong's Notices of the War of 1812*. Black Rock, U.S.A.: D.P. Adams, 1836.

Cruikshank, E.A. *Documentary History of the Campaign upon the Niagara Frontier*. 9 vols. Welland, Ont: Lundy's Lane Historical Society, 1896-1908.

———. *The Fight in the Beechwoods: a Study in Canadian History*. 2d. ed. Welland, Ont: Lundy's Lane Historical Society, 1895.

Dent, J.C. *The Story of the Upper Canadian Rebellion*. 2 vols. Toronto: C. Blackett Robinson, 1885.

Ewart, A., and Jarvis, J. "The Personnel of the Family Compact, 1791-1841", *Canadian Historical Review*, 7 (Sept. 1926), 209-21.

Fellowes, E.H. *The Military Knights of Windsor, 1352-1944*. Windsor, England: Oxley and Son, Ltd., 1944.

Firth, E.G., ed. *The Town of York, 1815-1834: A Further Collection of Documents of Early Toronto*. Toronto: The Champlain Society, 1966.

FitzGibbon, James. *An Appeal to the People of the Late Province of Upper Canada*. Montreal: Lovell and Gibson, 1847.

———. "The History of a Life", by an Old Soldier, *The London Review and Weekly Journal of Politics, Literature Art & Society*, 1 (21 July 1860), 62-63.

FitzGibbon, M.A. *A Veteran of 1812: The Life of James FitzGibbon*. Toronto: William Briggs, 1894.

Hitsman, J.M. *The Incredible War of 1812: A Military History*. Toronto: University of Toronto Press, 1965.

Jameson, Anna B. *Winter Studies and Summer Rambles in Canada*. 3 vols. London: Saunders and Otley, 1838.

Johnson, J.K. "Colonel James FitzGibbon and the Suppression of Irish Riots in Upper Canada", *Ontario History*, 58 (Sept. 1966), 139-55.

Joyce, P.W. *A Concise History of Ireland from the Earliest Times to 1922*. Dublin, Educational Company,n.d.

Kilbourn, William. *The Firebrand: William Lyon Mackenzie and the Rebellion in Upper Canada*. Toronto: Clarke, Irwin & Company, 1956.

Leighton, Douglas. "The Compact Tory as Bureaucrat: Samuel Peters Jarvis and the Indian Department, 1837-1845," *Ontario History*, 73 (March 1981), 40-53.

Lindsey, Charles. *The Life and Times of Wm. Lyon Mackenzie* . . . . 2 vols. Toronto: P.R. Randall, 1862.

Magill, M.L. "William Allan and the War of 1812", *Ontario History*, 64 (Sept. 1972), 132-41.

[Mackenzie, W.L.] *Mackenzie's Own Narrative of the Rebellion . . . in the Month of December 1837*. Toronto: Palladium Office, 1838.

McKenzie, Ruth. *Laura Secord: the Legend and the Lady*. Toronto: McClelland and Stewart, 1971.

Moir, J.S. "FitzGibbon's Secret Visitor", *Ontario History*, 48 (Summer 1956), 108-10.

Morris, A.Y. *Gentle Pioneers: Five Nineteenth-Century Canadians*. Toronto: Hodder and Stoughton, 1968.

Patterson, Graeme. "An Enduring Canadian Myth: Responsible Government and the Family Compact", *Journal of Canadian Studies*, 12, 2 (Spring 1977), 3-16.

Robertson, J.R. *The History of Freemasonry in Canada from its Introduction in 1749* . . . . 2 vols. Toronto: Morang, 1899.

Saunders, R.E. "What Was the Family Compact?", *Ontario History*, 49 (Autumn 1957), 165-78.

Scadding, Henry. *Toronto of Old*. Ed. and abr. by F.H. Armstrong. Toronto: Oxford University Press, 1966.

Senior, Hereward. "The Genesis of Canadian Orangeism", *Ontario History*, 60 (June 1968), 13-29.

Tupper, F.B., ed. *The Life and Correspondence of Major-General Sir Izaac Brock, K.B*. 2d. ed. London: Simpkin, Marshall & Co., 1847.

Valenti, N.C. "Cyrenius Chapin: Doctor and Pioneer", M.A. diss., Niagara University, Niagara Falls, N.Y., 1972.

Wise, S.F. "The Rise of Christopher Hagerman", *Historic Kingston*, 14 (1965), 12-23.

Index

www.ingramcontent.com/pod-product-compliance
Lightning Source LLC
LaVergne TN
LVHW050642100826
845148LV00011B/1948

* 9 7 8 0 9 1 9 6 7 0 7 1 6 *